THE WORLD'S STRIKE AIRCRAFT

UNIFORM WITH THIS BOOK

JOAN BRADBROOKE *The World's Helicopters*

H. F. KING *The World's Bombers*

H. F. KING *The World's Fighters*

JOHN STROUD *The World's Airliners*

JOHN STROUD *The World's Airports*

PUTNAM WORLD AERONAUTICAL LIBRARY

THE WORLD'S STRIKE AIRCRAFT

H. F. KING

THE BODLEY HEAD

LONDON SYDNEY TORONTO

ACKNOWLEDGMENTS

Thanks are due to the following for permission to quote extracts from copyright material: William Kimber & Co Ltd for the extract on pages 94–96 from *Phoenix Into Ashes* by Roland Beaumont; and Doubleday & Co Inc, New York, for the extracts on pages 21–22 from *Winged Warfare* by Major W. A. Bishop, VC, DSO.

ISBN 0 370 01571 1

Printed Offset Litho and bound in Great Britain for
The Bodley Head Ltd.
9 Bow Street, London WC2E 7AL
by Cox & Wyman Ltd, Fakenham
Set in Monotype Baskerville
First Published 1973

CONTENTS

INTRODUCTION

To strike a blow by hand or foot is the oldest form of attack in man's history: far older than the crudest weapons – the lump of wood, the sharpened stone or metal, the scalding liquid or the flying lead. For the close-in blow is one that registers as much by cunning and surprise as by force or weight. It is true that surprise may play a part however long the range, but in-fighting, to use a boxing term, leaves the shortest time for evasion or counter-blow.

More wars than one have shown that the heaviest bombardment, whether by long-range guns or high-flying bombers, can fail to eliminate a static strong-point in an army's path or a battleship in harbour. Swift, resolute surprise assault by low-flying aircraft can, on the other hand, achieve decisive results with far less weight of force and greater prospect of success.

Not without truth did Shakespeare declare: 'Thrice is he arm'd that hath his quarrel just'; but it was the great American humorist Artemus Ward who added so sagaciously: 'And four times he who gets his fist in fust'.

Although the motto of the Royal Navy's Fleet Air Arm is 'Find, Fix and Strike', the finding and the fixing (or the pin-pointing of the target) have generally been done from high level, whereas the strike with bombs, torpedoes or rockets has been the lot of dive-bombers, low-level bombers or torpedo-carriers. All these classes of aircraft we shall be meeting in this book, together with several other species which, although sometimes contrasting sharply with them, are designed or adapted for a similar purpose, namely that of trying to ensure a certain 'kill' by closing in on the target. Even the RAF's great V-bombers, which only a few years ago were charged with deterring a potential enemy by their high-flying ability and long-range 'stand-off' bombs, have, in the face of fast-growing effectiveness of anti-aircraft weapons, been reclassified in recent times as low-level attackers in the RAF's Strike Command.

Events and circumstances have so resolved themselves that it is almost true to say that the air arms of all the Powers exist in the recognition that offensive strength is most effectively exerted as it so

◀ A Hawker Hawfinch demonstrating, in the late 1920s, how a single-seat fighter might attack a ground target with its machine-guns.

often was in the First World War. Soon after that war was over the Air Minister of the day admitted publicly that in spite of improvements in bomb-sighting and diligence in practising with various forms of high-altitude attack, the only real way of making sure of hitting a target was still that of flying low and planting the bomb upon it.

True, it was largely the ineffectiveness of bomb-sights that was responsible for the state of affairs at that time, whereas it is now the growing potency of anti-aircraft defences which has so drastically re-shaped the tactics of modern offensive warfare. In the very early stages of the First World War bombing aircraft had to fly low in any case, for the simple reason that, when carrying any worth-while offensive load, they were quite unable to fly high. When it is recalled that the pilot of one of the Royal Flying Corps' earliest 'warplanes' was ordered to remove a light machine-gun from his Farman biplane because its weight would not enable him to climb high enough to shoot at the enemy aircraft he was trying to intercept, it will be understood that any appreciable weight of bombs imposed a far more severe penalty.

As engines began to give more power, and as aircraft design in general became more of a science than an art, so bombing aircraft began to operate at higher levels, largely because the hazards of gun-fire from the ground were thereby lessened. Even so, the advantages of low-level surprise attack quickly became apparent, and one of the earliest, most dramatic, and certainly most successful, raids of 1914 was that by a tiny Sopwith Tabloid biplane on a Zeppelin shed at Düsseldorf. From a height of about 600 ft (180 m) the pilot, Flt Lieut R. L. G. Marix, placed his tiny bombs with such effect that flames from the Zeppelin inside leaped up to within a hundred feet of the release height; but by then the Tabloid was well away, and ever since that time it has been a precept among ground-attack pilots to absent themselves without delay from whatever may be coming up from below, whether the enemy or they themselves are responsible.

It must, however, be made perfectly clear that the word 'strike' is not infrequently applied to attacks by high-flying bombers also: thus by 'bombing strike' may be implied a raid in force by aircraft of the class described strictly as bombers.

In *The World's Bombers*, the bomber was defined as 'An aeroplane designed or adapted for the primary purpose of delivering a bomb or bombs in level flight against non-specialised targets over medium and long distances'. Although high-level operation was implicit in the definition, there have been instances when special circumstances have dictated a low delivery height. The dam-busting operations by Lancasters in the Second World War, and the massive assault by American Liberators on the Ploesti oilfields in Rumania need only be instanced. In defining the classes of aircraft which form the subject-matter of the present volume, though the principle of low-level pin-point operation is common to them all, these are a very mixed bunch indeed.

A beginning might be made with those classes of aeroplane which were improvised for low-level attack, either because nothing else was available or because they were useless or deficient in their first-intended rôle. But this would be doing far less than justice to some of the later very highly specialised machines which answer to the title of strike aircraft; and although in a purely chronological sense these aircraft have their rightful place in the final chapters, they command first mention here by their sheer importance, for their military significance and technical interest alike. However, should it be judged from these remarks that the earlier types formed a sort of aeronautical rag-bag, then this will quickly be shown to be very far from the truth, for numbered among the earliest strike aircraft were some that were specialised to the point of extremity, and even, as we shall see, to over-extremity.

Before describing the development and characteristics of the aeroplanes concerned it must be emphasised that the particulars given in the tables of data are merely representative. This is necessarily so, because there were numerous variations in the dimensions, weights, performances and weapon loads of many of the types, especially those of later origin. In the tables 'torp' is used as the abbreviation for torpedo and guns are classified as 'm-g' (machine-gun) or cannon if measuring 15 mm or more in calibre or bore.

1

1914–18: Bullets and Bombs

The earliest aircraft used by the opposing Powers at the beginning of the 1914–18 war generally flew at low levels because they were unable to fly high, although that ability was an eminently desirable one not only in the interests of safety (avoiding ground fire, for instance, and enabling them to glide homewards should the engine fail, as it was very likely to do), but from a purely military standpoint also. The reason for this was that their primary tasks were not those of bombing or fighting but of reconnoitring for the infantry and spotting the fall of shot for the artillery. As early as 24 August 1914, during the first month of the war, France's great soldier Général Joffre had issued an order which he headed: *Note for all the Armies (instructions on tactics)*. The final paragraphs of this historic document read as follows:

'We must copy our adversaries in using aeroplanes to prepare artillery attacks.

'These aeroplanes fly over the ground, beyond the front, directing the artillery so that it can bring our assembled forces and our columns under its fire at maximum range, without our being able to determine, even approximately, the position of the batteries.'

Thus Général Joffre directed that the duties of the Allied aeroplanes were, first to discover targets, and second to give the artillery batteries the necessary information for directing their fire. This they often did by dropping messages in little bags.

The French, of course, had long been great artillery enthusiasts, especially since the days of Napoleon; but it did not require a mighty military brain to conceive the idea that aeroplanes themselves

◀ A new element of surprise was introduced into strike operations by fast fixed-wing aircraft capable of taking off and landing vertically, or, with increased load, of 'unsticking' after a slight forward run. The pre-eminent example of such an aircraft is the Hawker Siddeley Harrier, as shown.

This is not a picture of Marix attacking the Zeppelin shed, as related in the text, but the aircraft
is a Sopwith Tabloid of the type he used and a shed obliges in setting the scene.

could sometimes fulfil the functions of the guns. Some of the earliest French bombs were, in fact, nothing more or less than converted artillery shells. And so it came about that aeroplanes began to assume an offensive rôle by delivering 'strikes' against targets on the battlefield, and even beyond the enemy's lines, as witness the Düsseldorf raid by Flt Lieut Marix in October 1914. Nor was this the only one of its kind, for a few weeks afterwards, on 21 November 1914, three Avro 504 biplanes, originally designed (like the Sopwith Tabloid) with no warlike purpose in mind, struck at the Zeppelin sheds at Friedrichshafen.

In 1914 there was only the slenderest of hopes that an airship might be engaged in combat by an aeroplane, because of the lighter-than-air craft's ability to climb steeply and swiftly to heights beyond the aeroplane's attainment. The only really promising way of countering the menace of the Zeppelins was to destroy the monsters at their bases, and preferably, as Marix had shown, while in their sheds. Targets of this kind presented themselves along the Rhine; but these were out of reach by aeroplane, and the British Admiralty was fortunate in having an inviting and feasible objective in the Friedrichshafen Zeppelin works on Lake Constance. Even so, a raid on this centre would necessitate a flight of some 250 miles (400 km) over hostile terri-

tory, and preparations went ahead in the highest secrecy.

This was to be the first low-level strike by a group of aircraft in the history of military flying.

As the Avros' starting point, the town of Belfort, on the Franco-Swiss frontier, was chosen. Belfort was itself an airship base, and the great shed it possessed offered concealment of the aircraft from suspected spies. Lieut Noel Pemberton-Billing, who organised the raid, made the necessary arrangements with the French general in command.

The names of the pilots selected were Briggs, Babington, Sippé and Cannon, and, together with eleven mechanics, they left Southampton by sea on 10 November 1914. Bad weather delayed their great adventure, but on the 21st of the same month three of the four (Cannon's machine having broken its tailskid) set out.

From a height of about 5,000 ft (1,525 m) the raiders descended, to lessen the chances of perception and interception, until at last they were down to within 10 ft (3 m) of the surface of Lake Constance. This, indeed, was a low-level strike, as we would call it now; but Zeppelin sheds were tall, and the Avros arrived over Friedrichshafen at about 1,200 ft (365 m). Then once again they dived.

The full account of this audacious assault has never been told in the detail it deserves, for a long and terrible war still lay ahead, and perspectives changed as recollections faded. Stated briefly the results achieved were: one Zeppelin under construction severely damaged; one gasworks (for Zeppelin-filling) sent up in flames; one pilot (Briggs) forced to land by machine-gun fire – and met with an ugly reception!

It was the British pioneer airman A. V. Roe who designed the bomb-carriers for the Friedrichshafen raid. Improvised, perhaps, would be a more precise description, for Roe himself remarked that they were 'a Heath Robinson job'.

In the form of the low-level bomber the strike aeroplane was now a proven weapon; but, like the specialised torpedo-dropper, its initial success was not to be followed up by such successful exploits until some time had passed. This account of strike-aircraft development is, therefore, best resumed with a record of technical, rather than tactical, achievement.

One feature possessed in common by the later specialised strike aircraft was to be the built-in protection afforded for the crew-positions and other vital parts by heavy armour-plating; but even before war came in 1914 experiments were being made, both in Britain and in Europe, with high-resistance plates of steel. These were sometimes fitted, in the early phases of the conflict, to offer

An Avro 504 of the type used on the Friedrichshafen raid.

protection from rifle- and machine-gun fire delivered by the troops whose dispositions and movements were under observation; but there was at least one notable, if little known, instance of an aircraft having been armoured specifically for the attack of ground targets, and this was the much-maligned B.E.2c, designed at the Royal Aircraft Factory, Farnborough.

The unenviable reputation acquired by this aircraft was largely due to its stability, or power to right itself after disturbance from its course, a deliberate design feature to render it suitable for reconnaissance, but which, at the same time, made it unmanoeuvrable when attacked. Also, it was a difficult machine to fit with guns, although the large area of its wings enabled it to climb relatively high, and this redeemed its otherwise poor reputation by making it an effective destroyer of airships. The success which it achieved in this capacity has seldom been accorded the credit it so richly merits, this being mainly because it was the subject of a charge of criminal negligence made in the House of Commons early in 1916. This charge was levelled against the Higher Command of the Royal Flying Corps by none other than Noel Pemberton-Billing, whose name has already been mentioned as the organiser of the Friedrichshafen raid. 'I would suggest,' he said, 'that quite a number of our gallant officers have been rather murdered than killed.' The reason for this severe and dramatic accusation was the heavy losses sustained by the poorly armed and unmanoeuvrable B.E.2cs at the hands of the German fighter-pilots.

But the generous wing area which rendered the B.E.2c effective as an airship-killer also enabled it to lift a heavy load of armour plate – nearly 450 lb (205 kg), in fact; and, thus protected, it was used for ground strafing (the latter word was borrowed from the Germans themselves) in the Battle of the Somme during 1916. One example in particular, flown by a Capt Jenkins, must have received some sharp retaliation, for in a single three-month period it had to be fitted with no fewer than eighty new wings and numerous other components.

This special version of the B.E.2c may therefore be considered as the first British aeroplane to be adapted for low-level strikes against ground targets, though later in the war attacks of the same kind were made on the German trenches by another 'Factory' product, the F.E.8. This was the second and last of the British single-seat pusher fighters to be used on active service (the first having been the de Havilland D.H.2), and, having the engine and propeller at the rear, as the expression 'pusher' signifies, it afforded the pilot an excellent forward view. Armour protection was lacking, however.

In yet another product of the Royal Aircraft Factory both the pusher layout and protective armour were combined; and although only three examples were built, the type commands particular attention by reason of its specialised nature. This aeroplane appeared in 1918, and was known as the A.E.3 or the Farnborough Ram. The entire nacelle, or short fuselage which carried the crew and power-plant, was made of armour plate a quarter of an inch (6·35 mm) thick, and in the extreme nose was a specially designed mounting for twin Lewis machine-guns, the concentrated fire of which was to be directed by the gunner into the enemy's trenches, while the pilot, seated behind him, flew the aircraft low and level. A third Lewis gun was emplaced between the cockpits to give protective fire against aircraft attacking from the rear and above. But only three examples of this significant aeroplane were built, official attention being concentrated thereafter on the no-less specialised Sopwith Salamander later described.

Although designed specifically for combat in the air, certain earlier types of British single-seater were pressed into service to deliver small bombs against targets on the ground, as well as fire from their primary armament of machine-guns; and these were thus the true forerunners of the class of strike aircraft familiar today as the fighter bomber. Eminent among such aeroplanes was a fourth design by the Royal Aircraft Factory, and the most successful of them all: namely the S.E.5a. During 1917–18, fighting aircraft of this class were still called 'scouts', indicative of the intended function of what later became known as single-seat fighters and fighter bombers. The most notable action in which S.E.5a scout squadrons were employed to deliver four 20-lb bombs from each aircraft, in addition to bullets from their one Vickers gun and one Lewis gun, was the massive German offensive of March 1918, which the Allied armies failed to halt and for which the aid of the RFC was urgently requested. At that time the General Officer Commanding the RFC was Major-General Sir John Salmond, and on the 26th

of the month he issued the following order to all available squadrons, including those equipped with the S.E.5a. 'Bomb and shoot up everything you can see,' he said. 'Very low flying essential. All risks to be taken. Urgent.' So clearly was this order understood that a soldier of one German regiment later recorded: 'Several British Tommies flew so low that the wheels of their aeroplanes touched the ground. My company commander had to fling himself flat . . . but for all that he was struck on the back by the wheels of one of the machines, thus being literally run over.'

One famous S.E.5a squadron engaged in such hazardous operations was No.24, and between February and November 1918 this unit dropped no fewer than 2,229 bombs and fired 92,522 rounds of machine-gun ammunition at targets on the ground.

Nor were ground-attack operations by squadrons similarly equipped confined to the Western Front, for in his massive work *British Aeroplanes 1914–18* J. M. Bruce recorded: 'For the Palestine campaign, General Sir Edmund Allenby asked for a fighting squadron . . . This request was refused at the time (October 1917), but in January, 1918, No.111 was equipped with S.E.s; and by the time Allenby launched his final offensive No.145 Squadron was also in the field with six S.E.5as. The S.E.s of these two squadrons maintained standing patrols over the enemy aerodrome at Jenin, and kept the German pilots grounded. On 21 September, these S.E.5as took part in the annihilation of the Turkish Seventh Army in the Wadi el Far'a; two days later the machines of No.111 Squadron made similar attacks on the Turkish Fourth Army on the Es Salt–'Amman road'.

In actions such as these the fighter bomber proved its deadly effectiveness, especially against enemy troops and their transport, or what eventually became known as 'soft-skinned' vehicles. Not until a later period, when special weapons became available, were they to prove themselves as 'tank-killers'.

The remaining types of British aircraft to be considered in this chapter were the products of private companies, as were the Avro 504 and Sopwith Tabloid, which have already been mentioned. No later Avros command attention, but the name of Sopwith is one of continuing importance and technical significance, especially so in respect of the Salamander. In chronological sequence the Sopwith types extensively employed, or specifically designed, for ground attack, were the Pup, Camel, Dolphin, Snipe, Salamander and Buffalo.

The Pup, like the Camel, was essentially a single-seat fighter, but although it sometimes carried bombs in addition to its single machine-gun it is far less important than the Camel, a type strictly contemporary and comparable with the S.E.5a, but having a normal armament of two Vickers guns. For ground-attack work these were frequently supplemented (as on the S.E.5a and Pup, and on British single-seat fighters for many years to follow) by four 20-lb (9 kg) bombs. Earlier strikes against Zeppelin sheds were echoed by yet one more. On 19 July 1918 seven Camels attacked Tondern with heavier bombs, and according to one of the pilots engaged, who later became Marshal of the RAF Sir William Dickson, these were specially made 60-pounders (27 kg).

In the development of strike aircraft, however, the Camel has an even greater significance, for a special experimental 'armoured trench fighter' version was built early in 1918. On this aeroplane the armament was three Lewis guns, two firing downwards and the other forwards, as on the Pup, the standard Camel and S.E.5a. A sheet of armour-plate protected the pilot against fire from below.

The Dolphin and Snipe were both built essentially for combat in the air, and were merely adapted to carry light bombs as well as their forward-firing machine-guns; but even though the Salamander was a direct development of the Snipe it must now receive particular attention as the earliest type of British armoured ground-attack air-

Although the Sopwith Salamander greatly resembled the Snipe single-seat fighter, the entire forward fuselage was made of armour plate. Hence its angular appearance.

craft to be built in numbers, although it was never employed on active service.

The heavy armour-plating of the Salamander was its most notable and most familiar characteris-

tic, but a little-known fact is that this afforded protection not only by its resistance to machine-gun and rifle fire from the ground but by reason of the camouflage paintwork applied to it. For many years after the 1914–18 war the Salamander remained something of a mystery aeroplane because, although considerable numbers were built, these were retained in storage. At least one eye-witness account survives, however, and this records: 'The armour plating is painted in chocolate brown. On the wings is a forked-lightning camouflage design to render it comparatively invisible from above.' It was further remarked that no roundels, or circular national insignia, were carried, in order not to mar the camouflage effect.

Although in general appearance the Salamander resembled the Snipe, its fuselage was slab-sided instead of rounded, and the entire forward portion consisted of armour. Additional plating formed part of the covering round and behind the pilot's cockpit, as well as his padded head-rest, and the total weight of all this protection was nearly 650 lb (295 kg) – a heavy load indeed for a small aeroplane with an engine of only 230 hp. Added to this was the offensive load of two forward-firing Vickers machine-guns, each with 1,000 cartridges. This was an unprecedented ammunition supply for a pair of such guns, but bomb load remained as on the Snipe and other British single-seat fighters of 1918; namely four of 20 lb (9 kg).

The Buffalo was another Sopwith product of 1918, and was armoured much in the manner of the Salamander, although it was a two-seater with a defensive rear gun. The armour and armament carried by this aircraft would certainly have been used against any ground targets which presented themselves, but the Buffalo's primary purpose was what was known at the time as 'contact patrol': that is, to observe the positions of the opposing armies. It merits inclusion here for its low-flying tactics and its armour protection, and although never produced in quantity, it would have been used on active service had the Armistice not been signed.

The other British aircraft to be mentioned at this point were built by the Bristol, de Havilland, Martinsyde and Vickers companies. Uncommon among the fighting aeroplanes of the First World War in being a monoplane, the Bristol M.1C was also one of the fastest, having a top speed of about 130 mph (210 km/h). The true reasons why this remarkable aeroplane was never extensively employed for its intended purpose of air combat have never come to light, but on one occasion in the Middle East two aircraft of the type 'struck' in a novel manner by performing nerve-shattering low-level manoeuvres over some Kurdish tribesmen. Others of the same type attacked a big Turkish gun from a height of 200 ft (60 m) and silenced it.

Against ground targets the two-seat Bristol

Fighter had its fair share of action in low-flying attacks. It is recorded that Bristol Fighters manned by Australians 'exacted a dreadful toll of the retreating Turkish Seventh Army ... Trapped in the Wadi el Far'a, the Turks were systematically slaughtered in a day-long attack with bombs and machine-gun fire. In this grim work the Australians were helped by the S.E.5as of Nos.111 and 145 Squadrons, and by the D.H.9s of No.144 Squadron.'

The D.H.9 was of de Havilland origin but was primarily a high-altitude bomber pressed into service for an unintended purpose; whereas the D.H.5, a single-seat fighter, might be numbered among those aeroplanes mentioned earlier that were 'useless or deficient in their first-intended rôle'.

For various technical reasons the D.H.5 was never popular as a fighter, and certainly not at high altitudes; but it was very sturdy in construction, and as the top wing was behind the lower one, and the pilot was seated forward of it, he was afforded an exceptional field of view. These characteristics rendered the aircraft eminently suitable for diving attacks on ground targets, which included trenches, trench mortars and machine-gun emplacements. So specialised in such work did the type become that on arrival in France late in 1917 one particular squadron practised low-flying not only by individual aircraft but in formation also.

The Martinsyde Elephant was intended as a long-range fighter, but being sturdily constructed saw service also as a low-level bomber carrying relatively heavy loads. The Vickers Vampire was an experimental fighter converted for ground attack and having 500 lb (225 kg) of armour protection. To render the engine less vulnerable to gunfire from the ground the original water-cooled type was replaced by one cooled by air.

The concept of the fighting aircraft adapted for low-level attack with bombs as well as guns was essentially British, for although the French developed some excellent aircraft for aerial combat in the 1914–18 war they employed these with their normal armament of guns against ground targets. True, armour plating was being fitted to French military aircraft well before war came; but the idea of this was mainly to protect them from the fire of other machines, and their guns were for all-round use except downwards.

The types of French fighter employed extensively in action for low-level attacks were products of the Nieuport and SPAD concerns, and the most vivid account of a strike operation by a Nieuport *sesquiplane* ('one-and-a-half-winger') was given not by a French pilot but by the Canadian 'Billy' Bishop, whose total of victories in air combat was seventy-two. In 1918 Bishop wrote of an earlier exploit:

'My record of machines brought down was now in the vicinity of twenty, and I saw I had a rare chance of really getting a lot before going on my next leave . . .

'With this object in view I planned an expedition into the enemy country, to attack an aerodrome. I had carefully thought it out, and came to the conclusion that if one could get to an aerodrome when there were some machines on the ground and none in the air, it would be an easy matter to shoot them down the moment they would attempt to come up. It would be necessary for them to take off straight into the wind, if there was a strong wind at all, so I could not be surprised that way, and would be able to hit them if I came low enough before they would get a chance to manoeuvre or turn out of my way.

'Now came the day . . . I wrote my name on the blackboard to be called at 3 o'clock, and sat down for the last time to consider exactly if the job was worth the risk. However, as nothing like it had been done before, I knew that I would strike the Huns by surprise, and, considering that, I decided the risk was not nearly so great as it seemed, and that I might be able to get four or five more machines to my credit, in one great swoop.'

In the literature of air warfare this use of the word 'strike' to describe a low-level surprise attack must have been among the earliest.

A few glimpses of Bishop's historic attack convey a picture just as vivid as one later presented of a hardly less significant strike in the Second World War, when the aircraft concerned was not a frail little Nieuport but a massive Hawker Typhoon. So we continue in Bishop's own words:

'At 3 o'clock I was called . . . I got away just as the first streaks of dawn were showing in the upper sky.

'I flew straight across the lines, towards the aerodrome I had planned to attack, and coming down low, decided to stir them up with a burst of machine-gun fire into their hangar sheds. But, on reaching the place, I saw there was nothing on the ground. Greatly disappointed, I decided I would try the same stunt some other day.

'In the meantime I flew along low in the hope of coming on some camp or group of troops so as to scatter them . . . I was in rather a bad temper, and I was just thinking of turning and going home, or of climbing up to see if there were some Huns in the upper sky, when ahead, and slightly to one side of me, I saw the sheds of another aerodrome. I was not even certain where I was, and I was a bit afraid that if I had any bad fights I might have trouble in finding my way back. Scurrying along close to the ground, zigzagging here and there, one's sense of direction becomes slightly vague.

'I was over the aerodrome, about 300 ft (90 m) up. On the ground were seven German machines, and in my first glance I saw that some of them actually had their engines running . . .

'I pointed my nose towards the ground and opened fire with my gun, scattering the bullets all around the machines, and coming down to 50 ft (15 m) in doing so . . . I did my best to evade the fire from the ground . . . Then one machine suddenly began to "taxi" off down the aerodrome, and I immediately tore down after it. I managed to get close on its tail, when it was just above the ground, and opened fire from behind. There was no chance of missing. Just fifteen rounds, and it sideslipped, then crashed . . . I was now keyed up, and turning quickly, saw another machine just off the ground . . .'

This one Bishop sent crashing into some trees; but then his heart sank when he saw two machines taking off simultaneously. 'It was,' he recalled, 'the one thing I had dreaded'; but he managed to get in a short burst of fire on one, and this 'went crashing into the ground, where it lay in a field, only a few hundred yards from the aerodrome.'

Bishop concluded, 'I landed, and my sergeant rushed out and asked how many I had bagged.

When I told him three, he was greatly pleased . . . Then, as I crawled out of my machine, I heard the remarks of the mechanics. They were looking it over. Everywhere it was shot about, bullet-holes being in almost every part, although none, luckily, within 2 ft of where I sat.' That particular Nieuport took a great deal of repairing, but Bishop continued to fly it afterwards 'for pulling me through such a successful enterprise'. 'I personally congratulated the man who had charge of my gun, suddenly realizing that if it had jammed what a tight corner I would have been in.'

The trade of the 'man who had charge' of Bishop's Lewis machine-gun was, then as now, that of armourer, a term dating from centuries ago when the making of a warrior's weapons was one of the greatest military arts. In modern flying terminology an armourer maintains in serviceable order airborne weapons of many sorts, which, in the classes of strike aircraft remaining to be described, are of exceptional variety and interest.

To continue this present account of ground-attack aeroplanes of the First World War, we resume with the French SPADs – and with a reminder to the reader that the concept of the fighting aircraft adapted for low-level attack with bombs as well as guns was essentially British. For this reason, when SPADs came into British service, they had to be specially altered, and it is recorded that '. . . a container was evolved by the workshops of No. 19 Squadron which was fitted inside the fuselage behind the pilot'. This container held two 20-lb (9 kg) bombs only, since the usual British loading of four would have disturbed the balance of the French fighter; and the installation is of particular significance in being the first instance of internal bomb stowage on a single-seat low-level ground-attack aircraft.

A number of SPADs had as their armament (primarily for air combat) a cannon firing forward through the hollow shaft which carried the airscrew, or propeller; but the use of aircraft cannon against ground targets during the 1914–18 war was mainly confined to two-seat pusher biplanes generally employed for bombing or reconnaissance from high or medium levels. French examples were principally of Voisin design, but a little-known fact is that a few British F.E.2bs, of generally similar layout, attacked ground objectives with shell-firing 'pom-pom' cannon of a type used in the Boer War of 1899–1902. Trains were favourite targets, and darkness, rather than armour, gave protection.

Eminent among the fighters of 1914–18 that were used for ground-attack with their machine-guns were the German single-seat biplanes of Albatros, Fokker and Pfalz design, and among these the Pfalz D.III and D.XII were especially popular by reason of their sturdy construction for high-speed dives to low levels. German two-seaters employed for general purposes, including low-level attacks with bombs and guns, were of Albatros, Halberstadt and Rumpler design, and particular mention must be made of the Albatros C.III, which carried its small bombs in a cylindrical container between the cockpits – another early instance of internal stowage. The Halberstadt CL.II was likewise used on low-level 'close-support' operations on behalf of the German Army, but with its bombs externally stowed; and of greater significance were the Hannover two-seaters.

Among the German general-engineering firms which, at the Government's behest, adapted their facilities for aircraft production was the Hannoversche Waggonfabrik AG, specialising in the manufacture of railway rolling stock. During 1915–16 this company set to work making Aviatik, Rumpler and Halberstadt types under licence, but in 1917 they started construction of a notably compact two-seater for fighting and ground-attack. This was of their own design and was called the Hannover CL.II. Of composite (wood and metal) construction, this handy-looking two-seater entered service in December 1917, and nearly 450 examples were completed. Variants were the CL.III (80 built) and CL.IIIa (537 built). Contributing to the overall compactness of the design and to the extent of the gunner's field of fire was the short-span biplane tail. Armament was two machine-guns only; thus on ground-attack missions the manoeuvrability and the rear gun of the Hannover CLs were their principal assets.

One of the most remarkable aeroplanes of 1914–18, and one which might fairly be regarded as the first 'real' low-level strike landplane of all time, was the officially designated J.I (or J 4 according to Junkers' own system). Its nickname of Möbelwagen (furniture van) was suggested in part by its bulk and cumbersome appearance. Very extensive use of all-metal construction, the outcome of two years or more of pioneering work by the famous Junkers company, may have reinforced the same idea; and this particular 'furniture van' might well have been known in modern terminology as a security van, having heavy armour protection against ground fire as well as an offensive armament of two fixed forward-firing machine-guns and one free-mounted weapon of the same class. Size and weight inevitably detracted from manoeuvrability.

The first J.I was completed in the spring of 1917, the intended duties being not only low flying to ascertain the positions of forward troops but the attack of suitable targets. The type was a biplane

The relative size of the man standing by this Junkers J.1 armoured ground-attack aircraft helps to explain why this aeroplane was disrespectfully known as the 'furniture van'.

of unequal wing-span, its two thick wings, the uppermost of which measured 52 ft 6 in (16 m) in span, having no external bracing in the ordinary sense, though there was a system of struts close inboard to the fuselage, four of which joined the undercarriage attachment-points on the lower wing. This wing had only about one-third the area of the upper one.

Steel armour covered large sections of the fuselage, housing the engine, pilot, observer/gunner and petrol tank. The fuselage itself was hexagonal in section and tapered at its forward end to a neat spinner, or streamlined hub-cover for the airscrew of the 200 hp Benz engine. The elegance of this feature was unhappily marred by obtrusive 'chimney stack' exhaust pipes. The total weight of the armour-plate was over 1,000 lb (450 kg), and some aircraft of the type carried machine-guns additional to the normal ones. These fired forward and downward through holes in the armour.

Nearly 230 J.Is were completed at the Junkers Dessau works and were used not only for the purposes stated but for medium-altitude observation also, and even photographic reconnaissance, for they were far less vulnerable to gunfire than types more generally employed for these purposes.

	Span	Length	Crew	Loaded weight	Maximum speed	Armament
GREAT BRITAIN						
Sopwith Tabloid	25' 6"	20' 4"	1	1,120 lb	92 mph	20-lb bombs (number uncertain)
Avro 504	36' 0"	29' 5"	1	1,575 lb	80 mph	4×20-lb bombs
Sopwith Salamander	31' 3"	19' 6"	1	2,512 lb	125 mph	2 m-g+4×20-lb bombs
GERMANY						
Hannover CL.II	39' 4"	25' 5"	2	2,440 lb	103 mph	2 m-g+small bombs
Junkers J.I	52' 6"	29' 10"	2	4,795 lb	97 mph	3 m-g

m-g=machine-gun

The Sopwith Cuckoo, the war-load installation of which is seen in close-up, was the world's first torpedo-dropper with wheel undercarriage designed to operate from an aircraft-carrier.

2

The Coming of Torpedoes: Great Britain, Germany, Italy

The early history of torpedo-dropping aeroplanes has been frequently presented not only inexactly but confusingly; so it must now be made clear that the true pioneers of this technique were the Italians. The man chiefly concerned was General A. Guidoni, who, not very many years before the Second World War, gave this account:

'I was ordered in 1912 to help Mr Pateras Pescara, who had suggested to the navy the building of a torpedo-plane. Mr Pescara was a lawyer. Had he been a technical man he would probably have been refused permission to try out his scheme . . . With my faithful Farman I succeeded in dropping 170 lb (77 kg), so I concluded that with a machine of 6,000 lb (2,720 kg) total weight it would be pos-

sible to drop a small torpedo.' A special twin-engined monoplane was accordingly built, and of this the general recalled: 'With this machine in February 1914 I succeeded in dropping a torpedo of 750 lb (340 kg), and perhaps this can be considered as the first torpedo launch.'

That this was indeed the first torpedo launch, or drop, from an aircraft of any kind is now beyond doubt, but the scene of practical development soon changed to Calshot in Britain. Here, in July 1914, trials were made with the dropping from a Short seaplane, never intended for the task, of a Naval-type Whitehead torpedo measuring 14 inches (35·5 cm) in diameter and weighing about 900 lb (408 kg).

The first torpedo attacks by aircraft in actual warfare were likewise British accomplishments, and the aircraft concerned were again Short seaplanes. These, however, had been specially designed for torpedo-launching and were officially designated Admiralty Type 184, though they were more familiar as the 'Short "Two-two-five"', by reason of their Sunbeam engine's horsepower.

In June 1915 the seaplane-carrying ship *Ben-my-Chree* arrived in the Eastern Mediterranean to participate in what is now famous in military history as the Dardanelles campaign. She carried three Type 184s, and on 12 August one of these seaplanes, piloted by Flight-Commander C. H. K. Edmonds, took-off with its torpedo to attack enemy shipping. Although no observer was carried in the rear cockpit, the aircraft could climb no higher than 800 ft (240 m), but on sighting a large steamer Edmonds glided down to a mere 15 ft (4 m) or so above the water and from a range of 300 yd (275 m) released his 'fish', as the torpedo became known in naval/air slang. It struck the target squarely, and although it later transpired that the ship concerned had already been put out of action by a British submarine this was quite literally the first 'torpedo strike' in aeronautical history. On 17 August Edmonds actually sank a Turkish ship from a range of 800 yd (730 m), and on the same day Flt Lieut G. B. Dacre

torpedoed and sank a large steam tug.

Throughout the 1914–18 war Britain continued to develop torpedo-dropping aircraft, all the earliest of which were seaplanes and were handicapped accordingly not only by the weight of the torpedo but by the float undercarriage also. The next type worthy of mention is the Short Type 320 (the figure once again denoting engine horsepower). This increased power, compared with that available to the 'Two-two-five', was welcome not only in the interests of performance generally but because the torpedo carried was increased in diameter from 14 in to 18 in (35·5 to 45·75 cm) and weighed 1,000 lb (450 kg). The pilot sat in the rear of the two cockpits, and when the torpedo was carried he was the sole occupant of the aircraft. For reconnaissance or bombing, however, provision was made for an observer/gunner: he stood on the sides of his cockpit, just ahead of the pilot's, to fire his Lewis machine-gun from a mounting level with the top-wing – a draughty business.

Several attempts were made to use seaplanes of this type in action, including one operation in which they were carried on special rafts towed by motor launches, the purpose being to increase the flying range of the seaplanes, already heavily laden with their torpedo and petrol load; but no successes against enemy shipping were achieved by this otherwise notable Short product.

Torpedo-dropping aeroplanes are mainly associated with aircraft-carriers; and rightly so, for coastal defence by such machines flying from land bases has generally been a secondary consideration. The first aeroplane of the class to be operated, with wheel undercarriage, from an aircraft-carrier's deck was the Sopwith Cuckoo; and thus the firm of Sopwith re-enters the story of strike aircraft in one more important respect.

The history of the Cuckoo is a fascinating one, and the aircraft's name was derived in part at least from the fact that the Cuckoo was 'designed to lay its eggs in other people's nests'. It is significant that this particular Sopwith 'bird' was developed and put into production by the Blackburn company, whose name thereafter was to become pre-eminent in the development of torpedo-dropping aeroplanes.

Although design of the Cuckoo was started in 1916, construction of the first experimental model was delayed. During a visit to the Sopwith works in February 1917, Wing Commander A. M. Longmore (later Air Chief Marshal), who had himself made the first torpedo-drop from a British aircraft at Calshot in 1914, saw part of the unfinished machine slung from the beams of one of the workshops. At his instigation work was restarted, and 350 examples were eventually ordered. Of these, ninety had been delivered when the Armistice was signed, but none was ever in action.

One technical feature of the Cuckoo meriting special mention was its 'split' undercarriage, which means that there was no axle between the two wheels to interfere with the release of the torpedo. An experimental British torpedo-dropper of about the same period – the Blackburn Blackburd – was to release its wheeled undercarriage entirely before attacking its target, the idea being to land back aboard the carrier on skids or 'ditch' in the sea.

The next torpedo-dropper to enter British service was the Blackburn Dart, a single-seater like the Cuckoo, but capable of carrying heavy bombs as an alternative load to the torpedo, and accordingly officially classified as a torpedo-bomber. Strictly, the term should have been unhyphenated, for otherwise it might have been supposed that the Dart was intended to bomb torpedoes, instead of release them. That a British aeroplane did, on one occasion, actually bomb a torpedo is a little-known fact, and the circumstances were as follows.

One day in the 1920s the pilots of some Darts were good-humouredly bragging about the potency of their torpedoes and the difficulty of deflecting or avoiding these once they were set on course for the target. Among the audience of RAF army co-

A Blackburn Dart drops its torpedo.

operation pilots was one who had notions of his own, and in a trial next day he contrived to deposit a bomb so neatly that one air-launched torpedo at least never found its mark.

This literally diverting little anecdote presents an opportunity to explain the use in this book of the term torpedo-dropping, as distinct from torpedo-carrying, aeroplane, though the latter is far more

commonly employed. One of the reasons for this explanation is again little-known, but nevertheless of interest and importance, and it is merely this: that although a few big flying-boats (notably the Italian Savoia Marchettis later mentioned) made actual use of the torpedo as a weapon of attack, it was a British practice at about the same period to move a torpedo from one place to another by carrying it as 'deck cargo' on top of a flying-boat hull. Many historical inaccuracies have arisen for this reason.

The present survey of British torpedo-dropping aircraft continues with the Blackburn Ripon and Baffin, which entered service respectively in the early and mid-1930s. Both were essentially the same, but the Baffin had an air-cooled Bristol Pegasus engine instead of a water-cooled Napier Lion as in the Dart and Ripon. The Ripon especially represented a significant technical advance, for not only was there a second crew-man to observe, assist in navigation and give protection with his machine-gun, but the pilot had a machine-gun also.

To replace the Baffin, and further to extend the capabilities of the carrier-borne torpedo-dropping aircraft, it was decided to introduce a new class of machine known as the T.S.R., signifying that, in addition to torpedo-dropping, the specified duties were 'spotting' the fall of shot for the big guns of the Fleet, and reconnaissance. Two types of aircraft, the Blackburn Shark and Fairey Swordfish, were ordered in numbers to meet this requirement, and although the Swordfish was to achieve by far the greater fame, it is now appropriate to deal with the Shark as the Blackburn successor to the Baffin and then to consider the later products of the same pioneering company.

Technically, the Shark had at least one feature of uncommon interest, for although several types of carrier-borne aircraft, both earlier and later, had air-bags to keep them afloat in case of a ditching, its metal fuselage was watertight. During the war of 1939–45 the Blackburn company built Swordfish under licence (just as it had formerly built Sopwith Cuckoos), and the next all-Blackburn carrier-borne torpedo-dropper was the single-seat Firebrand, originally built as a fighter in 1942, but developed to

Although a single-seater, the Blackburn Firebrand, was quite a massive aeroplane, nearly 40 ft long. This fact gives scale to the torpedo.

take a torpedo as its primary weapon. In a military sense the Firebrand was unimportant, for it did not enter service until the war was over; in a technical sense its special Blackburn torpedo-carrier is worthy of mention, for, being adjustable, it allowed the 'fish' to be carried horizontally for minimum air-resistance in flight or to be set nose-down for release, or for the tail to clear the ground or deck.

The Firebrand's successor was not a Blackburn aircraft; it was designed and built by the Westland company, and named the Wyvern. It was largely comparable in being a massive-looking single-seater which was never in action, except at Suez in 1956; but this was the first torpedo-dropper to use as its powerplant the propeller-turbine, closely related to the turbojet (or jet engine as it is popularly called), but with the gas-turbine driving a propeller instead of helping to create a propulsive jet. The Wyvern was an aggressive-looking machine, especially so as it had two big propellers mounted one behind the other and rotating in opposite directions; but historically it is important here only because it used a new form of engine.

On the other hand, the Fairey Swordfish (already mentioned jointly with the Blackburn Shark) represented no remarkable technical advance whatever, though in the annals of naval/air warfare it ranks among the most famous aircraft of all time. This is

due in part to the fact that it proved unusually adaptable for duties that were never specified in the original 'operational requirement', as represented by the designation T.S.R. Here this famous aeroplane is considered in its primary function as a torpedo-dropper.

The 'Stringbag', as the Swordfish came to be known in later years by reason of its antiquated biplane structure, with numerous struts and bracing-wires, dated from an experimental Fairey type of 1933. The importance in a carrier-borne torpedo-dropper of a good field of view for the pilot had long been recognised, both for landing on the deck and for delivering the attack, and an early Fairey document declares: 'The pilot's view has been very carefully studied, and the centre-section struts have been brought to an inverted V in front of the windscreen . . . The centre-section has been designed and positioned to give the minimum interference during the dive down to the dropping height, when the strut arrangement gives a sighting view of the target which is completely free from obstruction.'

No further comment on this description is necessary, except to explain that the 'centre-section' was the portion of the top wing which remained fixed when the outer sections were folded back for easy stowage below an aircraft-carrier's deck, and that the 'dropping height' was a few feet above the water.

Of all the wartime exploits of the Swordfish, the attack on the Italian fleet at Taranto in November 1940 was the best known. By the light of flares, in face of daunting hazards, not the least of which were barrages of guns and balloon cables and anti-torpedo nets, the 'Stringbags' struck. Numerous ships were sunk or damaged and the balance of naval power was vastly altered at a critical phase of the war by a small force of elderly strike aircraft.

The need for a Swordfish replacement had been clearly apparent before war came in 1939, and the Fairey company's answer was the Albacore, a far more modern-looking machine having refinements such as enclosed cockpits, and flaps on the wings which could be used not only to reduce landing speed but to restrict the speed in a bombing dive, for the techniques of dive-bombing (see Chapter 5) were very well established when the new type was designed and tested in the late 1930s. As an alternative load to the torpedo suspended under the fuselage, bombs could be carried under the wings as on the Dart, Ripon, Baffin, Shark, Swordfish, Firebrand and Wyvern. Yet in spite of its general modernisation the Albacore was still a biplane, and although intended to replace the Swordfish it came to be regarded more as a supplementary type. Eight hundred Albacores were built, and the action at Cape Matapan in March 1941 can be listed high among the type's battle honours.

The first British monoplane requiring description is the Albacore's descendant, the Barracuda. In all essentials this new Fairey product was clean-cut in appearance, but among the items which marred its lines was the blister-like 'radome', for by the time it was established in service, during 1943, radar for locating targets was coming into widespread use. Bombs, mines or depth charges were alternative loads to the torpedo, and as a dive-bomber, rather than as a torpedo-dropper, this type achieved its greatest fame.

An intended Barracuda replacement was the de Havilland Sea Mosquito, but its main claim to distinction here is that it was the first twin-engined torpedo-dropper to land aboard an aircraft-carrier. The date was 25 March 1944.

It was remarked earlier that coastal defence by torpedo-dropping aeroplanes flying from land bases was generally a secondary consideration to their employment from aircraft-carriers; yet Great Britain, among other nations, developed land-based types and put them into service. Several prototypes, or experimental models, were built, and one in particular, the Blackburn Cubaroo of 1924, calls for mention in that it was one of the largest single-engined aeroplanes ever built, and carried a torpedo not of 18-in (47·75 cm) diameter, as was usual, but a special 21-in (53·33 cm) Admiralty type weighing about 1½ tons (1,525 kg).

The Hawker Horsley was the first aircraft of this class to come into British service, during 1928. It was adapted from a standard type of RAF bomber of

Manoeuvrability was a very great asset in a torpedo-dropping aeroplane, especially in escaping after the torpedo had been released. This Hawker Horsley demonstrates its capabilities with the weapon still in place.

The Coming of Torpedoes: Great Britain, Germany, Italy

the same name, and continued in use until replaced by the Vickers Vildebeest in 1933.

The Air Ministry officially decreed that Vildebeest should be spelt without a final 'e', and some well-known history books which err in this regard nevertheless record the gallant, if ineffectual, actions of these obsolete biplanes during the Japanese invasion of Singapore in 1941.

Well before the Japanese assault, Britain had declared war on Germany, and of the first British bombing raid against that country, in September 1939, the leader, Flt Lieut K. C. Doran, recorded:

'The war was only 24 hours old, but already the bomb load had been changed four times. Lunchtime on the 4th September found us standing by at an hour's readiness, the Blenheims bombed-up with 500-lb (225 kg) S.A.P. Suddenly we got more "gen". Units of the German Fleet had been sighted . . .' Having described in an appropriate term the weather which appeared to be prevailing in the Heligoland Bight, Doran continued: '. . . the only attack possible would be a low-level one. We could not carry torpedoes, so off came the 500-lb S.A.P. and on went 500-lb with 11 seconds delay fuse.'

This account is of special interest in the present narrative for several reasons. First, the employment of bombers intended mainly for high-altitude operation on a low-level strike. Second, the term S.A.P., meaning semi-armour-piercing, or for special use against warships. Last, the eleven-second delay in the fusing of the 'general-purpose' bombs actually used, affording the Blenheims that space of time to clear the target area.

That the Blenheim could not carry torpedoes is not surprising, for it was never intended to do so; but only four months or so were to elapse before the introduction into RAF service of a new type of land-based torpedo-dropper. Like the Blenheim, this was a Bristol design but it differed extensively and was named the Beaufort.

Not only was this new aeroplane the RAF's first shore-based torpedo-dropper to have two engines – mounted on the wings, and thus not interfering with the pilot's view for torpedo-aiming; but, as a second innovation, the weapon itself was stowed semi-internally. These same technical features were also to be seen in a more-or-less contemporary and comparable type, the Blackburn Botha; but although built in considerable numbers, this was an inferior aeroplane, and as its designer once remarked: 'The original specification was intended for comparatively short-range operation. The collapse of France made this short range inadequate and its rôle was changed to an operational trainer for bomber crews.'

Although the Beaufort had disappeared from

Although in this particular picture the Vickers Vildebeest torpedo-dropper responsible for the splash in the foreground is somewhat indistinct, the size of the splash itself bears witness to the bulk of the 18-inch projectile.

first-line service by 1944, it gave a good account of itself in action, not only over the English Channel, North Sea and Atlantic, but the Mediterranean also; and in addition to well over 1,000 built in the United Kingdom, Australia constructed another 700, powered with American engines. The armament of machine-guns was a heavy one for such an aircraft, but was mainly for defence. As for offensive load, various combinations of bombs could be carried up to a normal weight of 1,500 lb (680 kg), though in May 1940 a Beaufort became the first British torpedo-dropper to release a 2,000-lb (907 kg)

The twin-engined Bristol Beaufort was built under licence in Australia, as betokened by this photograph, the setting of which calls for no further comment.

bomb. The primary weapon was, however, a torpedo, stowed semi-internally, and here it must be emphasised that, as was the case with all torpedo-dropping aircraft of this period, the bomb load was alternative, and not additional to, the 'fish'. This emphasis seems necessary because one quite well-known picture of a Vildebeest, having an imposing-

looking array of bombs under the wings as well as the torpedo under the fuselage, is sometimes described as showing 'full war load'.

Seemingly curious, perhaps, is the fact that, whereas the Beaufort carried its torpedo semi-internally, on its replacement type in RAF Coastal Command service – the closely related Beaufighter –

the weapon was slung externally beneath the fuse-lage, much as on the old Vildebeest, and even the Cuckoo of 1917. But, as the Beaufighter's name suggests, it was intended for air combat, and favourite targets for the first of the 'Coastal Beaus' (the nickname 'Torbeau' followed adaptation for torpedo-dropping) were German aeroplanes over the Bay of Biscay. Yet even with torpedo in place, the Beaufighter was much faster than its predeces-sor; so much so, in fact, that the last of the torpedo-dropping versions had bellows-like air-brakes on the wings to reduce the speed of approach to the target to one more suitable for the actual drop.

By the time the Beaufighter had completed its service with Coastal Command, some years after the war was over, it had struck at various targets with torpedoes, bombs, cannon and rocket projec-tiles; but though this present chapter is mainly concerned with torpedoes one can hardly fail to add that, in June 1942, a 'Coastal Beau' hedge-hopped to Paris in daylight, dropped a tricolour over the Champs Elysées, and got in a burst of cannon-fire at the German Admiralty Headquarters before returning home. Thus does the Beaufighter rank high among low-level aircraft.

In stress of war all kinds of aircraft have been called upon for services not only beyond the pilots' call of duty but beyond the intentions – and even dreams – of their designers. Torpedo-dropping, for instance, was never among the functions foreseen for the famous Vickers Wellington and Handley Page Hampden twin-engined bombers, yet torpedo-armed Wellingtons operated from Malta against Axis shipping, and Hampdens were found even wider employment with the same capability. Several even went to Russia, flying from a base near Murmansk; and others patrolled the North Sea. Conversely, the Bristol Brigand, designed specifi-cally to replace the torpedo-dropping Beaufighter, rendered its greatest service during 1950–54 against terrorists in Malaya, using bombs and rocket pro-jectiles.

It was, in fact, in Germany as early as 1915 that the first land-based torpedo-dropper was built. This was the Albatros B.IIT, and was thus much earlier even than Britain's carrier-borne Cuckoo, though Germany was never to use aircraft-carriers as warships.

During 1916 experiments were undertaken with various types of torpedoes and aircraft to drop them, and a special lightweight weapon made of bronze instead of steel was developed for single-seat shore-based machines. Seaplanes came next under review, but as a crew of two was required in addition to the war load it was considered that two engines were likewise needful. A German officer once wrote of the 'Torpedo-Plane Flight' stationed at Zeebrugge, and which became active in March 1916: 'The flight was equipped with five twin-engined machines of the Gotha type ... These machines behaved well in the air, and in calm water (in the lee of the Mole at Zeebrugge) they took off very well. In a rough sea they could only start and alight at great risk ...

'Attacks were almost always undertaken in misty weather, and when clouds were low, and mostly only by two machines, which, flying in the lower cloud layer, surprised and attacked English merchant steamers between Dover and Yarmouth.'

The first successful German torpedo attack on Allied shipping occurred on 9 November 1916, when a steamer was sunk off the Thames estuary; but as the war developed so did German interest in this form of attack decline to the point of virtual abandonment, for losses in men and machines had been high and effectiveness low. Mention is nevertheless called for, of the Brandenburg GW, another big seaplane which served with the Gotha.

That the German and British torpedoes often failed to run true is not surprising, for even by this time the techniques of dropping, and the modifications necessary to enable the weapons to be launched by an aeroplane rather than a ship, were very imperfectly understood. Yet between the wars

As explained in the text, the Heinkel He 115 was so efficient that, in specially prepared form, it gained speed records for aircraft of its class. Here it is seen in operational trim, with torpedo-bay doors clearly visible.

the Germans continued to develop torpedo-dropping seaplanes, of which the Dornier Do D and Do 22 were single-engined and of only passing interest. Such was not the case with the Heinkel He 59 and He 115, for not only were these larger, twin-engined machines, built in far bigger numbers, but their technical and operational history was incomparably more significant.

Production of the He 59 – a biplane – began in 1932, as a torpedo-dropper and general-purpose anti-shipping aircraft for the still-clandestine Luft-waffe. It saw active service in the Spanish Civil War, but in the greater war to follow was so out-dated in design that it served mainly for mine-laying, training and air/sea rescue work. Among torpedo-droppers, on the other hand, the He 115 monoplane was a technical classic, and on 20 March 1938 a specially prepared specimen captured eight inter-national speed records for seaplanes of its weight class. These were established without such speed-reducing military installations as defensive gun-positions; but the torpedo itself was an item which created no 'aerodynamic drag', or air resistance, for it was carried inside the slender fuselage. It is as a layer of magnetically operated mines rather than as a torpedo-dropper that the He 115 is, perhaps, better remembered.

By far the most numerous and effective torpedo strikes by German aircraft in the 1939–45 war were made by adapted twin-engined bombers. Chief among these were the Heinkel He 111 and Junkers Ju 88, though in some instances the Dornier Do 217, which was principally famous as an anti-shipping aircraft by reason of the guided weapons which it launched, had its internal bomb-compartment lengthened by several feet to accommodate a torpedo.

Just as in 1916, during 1940 the Germans under-took a series of trials to determine the most suitable shore-based aircraft available for torpedo-dropping, and the choice fell immediately on the He 111. Accordingly, among the war loads of the He 111 H-6, by far the most widely used of all the versions of this historic aeroplane, were two LT F5b tor-pedoes, carried externally, one on each side between the engines and fuselage. The letters LT signified Lufttorpedo, or air-launched torpedo, the French equivalent being aérotorpille.

Operating together, He 111s and Ju 88s struck with terrible effect against Allied shipping sailing in convoy via the Arctic to Murmansk and Archangel. Of these two types of aircraft the Ju 88 was the smaller, faster and more manoeuvrable, though its two torpedoes were externally slung as on the Heinkel. As a bomber, however, the Ju 88 achieved its greatest fame on anti-shipping strikes.

Among experimental German torpedo-droppers was a version of the Focke-Wulf Fw 190 fighter – recalling the fact that the very earliest torpedo-droppers were likewise single-seaters, for the compelling reason that they were unable to add further to their already heavy burden. The Fw 190, on the other hand, was only a fraction of their size, carried a torpedo weighing more than twice as much, and (very comforting to the sole occupant, especially after attacking) was more than four times as fast.

Twin hulls, allowing a torpedo to be slung between them, distinguished the
Italian Savoia Marchetti S.55 flying-boat.

We must now take up once again the story of Italian developments following the achievement of Guidoni in February 1914.

That the Italians were pioneers (after the Russians) in developing very large aeroplanes intended for bombing was made apparent in *The World's Bombers*. The Caproni Ca 33, as there described, operated also with the Italian Navy for torpedo-dropping, and another Caproni which saw service in the same, though more limited, capacity was the Ca 43 seaplane. This was not only encumbered by its floats but by its towering triplane wing structure,

and, like all big weight-lifters of its time, and for many years to follow, presented an inviting target to opposing gunfire, not by its bulk alone, but by its incapacity for swift manoeuvre.

The same was true of another Italian torpedo-dropper dating from 1924. This was the Savoia Marchetti S.55, a twin-hulled flying-boat monoplane which, although it had its two engines set one behind the other in tandem instead of side by side, still presented a sizeable target when viewed head-on, as by the anti-aircraft gunners on ships.

The S.55 achieved world fame for its participation in transocean mass formation flights in the early 1930s when led by General Italo Balbo, and it was used in numbers as a civil airliner.

Although the S.55 achieved no enduring fame as a torpedo-dropper, its original purpose being almost entirely forgotten, this was far from being the case with its very much faster and more manoeuvrable landplane successor, the S.M.79. This had an engine in the nose as well as two on the wings, and was thus of a general class much favoured by the Italians, yet the pilot, being seated at the front end of a characteristic hump, the rear of which housed one of the two defensive gunners, was little impeded in his view for torpedo-dropping.

The first flight of the S.M.79 came about ten years later than that of the S.55, but by the end of its ten-year term of first-line service some 1,200 examples of this aggressive-looking *trimotore* monoplane had been completed. As a bomber the type saw active service in the Spanish Civil War, but torpedo-dropping trials did not begin until November 1937. Typical loads in the Second World War were one or two torpedoes, slung beneath the fuselage, and this was likewise the case with a refined development, the S.M.84, which entered more limited service in 1941.

The monoplane formula was eventually adopted by Caproni, a company which in earlier years had favoured biplanes and even triplanes. But the Caproni monoplane torpedo-droppers may be dismissed with the observation that they were not outstanding performers, being too closely related to low-powered types intended primarily for general service in the Italian colonies.

The Cantieri Riuniti dell'Adriatico (Cant) was founded in 1923 as a subsidiary to a famous firm of shipbuilders, and, not surprisingly, marine aircraft were the company's primary concern. The type which first commands attention here was, in fact, a twin-float seaplane much in the style of the German He 115, but larger, and followed Italian fashion in having three engines. Known as the Cant Z.506B, it carried its torpedo in a long bulge under the fuselage, and at the rear end of this was a defensive machine-gun position. A landplane counterpart, though much faster in the absence of floats, was the Z.1007bis. Though this could carry two torpedoes, these were slung externally as the fuselage was slender. Having a fuselage very much larger in cross-section, the four-engined Piaggio P.108B, Italy's largest bomber of the Second World War, could carry no fewer than three torpedoes internally; and at the opposite end of the size scale was an experimental torpedo-dropping version of the Reggiane Re 2002 single-seat fighter. The torpedo was slung externally under the fuselage.

	Span	Length	Crew	Loaded weight	Maximum speed	Armament
GREAT BRITAIN						
Sopwith Cuckoo	46′ 9″	28′ 6″	1	3,875 lb	103 mph	1 torp
Blackburn Dart	45′ 6″	35′ 6″	1	6,400 lb	110 mph	1 torp or bombs
Blackburn Ripon	44′ 10″	36′ 9″	2	7,405 lb	126 mph	1 torp or bombs+2 m-g
Fairey Swordfish	45′ 6″	36′ 4″	2–3	9,250 lb	139 mph	1 torp or bombs+2 m-g
Bristol Beaufort	57′ 10″	44′ 7″	4	21,228 lb	265 mph	1 torp or bombs+3 m-g
GERMANY						
Heinkel He 115	73′ 1″	56′ 9″	3	22,928 lb	203 mph	1 torp or bombs+2 m-g
ITALY						
Savoia Marchetti S.55	79′ 11″	54′ 2″	6	16,975 lb	146 mph	1 torp or bombs+4 m-g
Cant Z.506B	86′ 11″	63′ 1″	4	28,000 lb	217 mph	1 torp or bombs+3 m-g

torp = torpedo   m-g = machine-gun

3

The Coming of Torpedoes: USA, Japan, USSR, France, Netherlands

The United States showed a very early interest in torpedo-dropping aircraft, proposals for which had been made well before 1914. Before describing the development of American torpedo-droppers, which advanced in design efficiency much in parallel with the US Navy's aircraft-carriers, we may note the words of Admiral Sims, usn, who forecast in 1921 that such craft '. . . will sweep the enemy fleet clean of its airplanes and proceed to bomb the battleships and torpedo them with torpedoplanes. It is all a question as to whether the airplane carrier is not the capital ship of the future.' Such, indeed, it became; and eminent among its complement of aircraft were the torpedo-droppers.

At about the time Admiral Sims was making

these observations the US Navy was evaluating the British Blackburn Swift, from which the Dart had been developed. But although the Swift was purchased as being the most technically advanced aircraft of its day, the Americans had already been working along lines of their own. Thus, shortly after the Armistice of 1918, studies were made of several possible types of aircraft, both existing and projected, and a few Curtiss R-6 biplanes were actually tested as torpedo-droppers. These, however, proved too frail for their exacting task, entailing, as it did, lifting and diving with a heavy load, and by 1921 further development work was being undertaken by the Naval Aircraft Factory. The outcome was a hybrid, the pedigree of which has no significance

here, called the PT-1, and in slightly modified form the PT-2. Of these two types of biplane thirty-three were delivered to the US Navy, the first of them in October 1921.

During this same year three experimental torpedo-droppers – the first military aeroplanes to bear the world-renowned name of Douglas – were ordered by the Navy under the designation DT-1. Ready interchangeability of a wheel undercarriage or floats was a particular feature, and sizeable orders followed for successively improved versions. Indicative of the lifting powers of the torpedo-dropping class of aircraft, whether in the form of its heavy and deadly weapon or special provisions for long-range flying without military load, was the first round-the-world flight, made (in stages) during 1924 by four Douglas World Cruisers. These historic aeroplanes were essentially similar to the DT-2 torpedo-dropper; and it may be added here that during 1927 a specially prepared Hawker Horsley, a British type already mentioned, unofficially held the world's long-distance record, though for two hours only – until surpassed by Lindbergh's non-stop New York–Paris flight!

The name of Curtiss was world-famous long before Douglas or Hawker were ever heard of, and the old R-6s having already been accorded their place, the Curtiss CS-1 of 1923 now calls for atten-

tion – if only for the facts that its top wing was shorter than the bottom one and that the Martin company was chosen to build the type in quantity, together with a slightly different model. This was merely because Martin entered a lower bid for the work than did Curtiss themselves; yet in its own right this other famous American constructor was already in the torpedo-dropping business, and it came to pass as follows.

The big twin-engined Martin bombers were well to the fore from 1918 onwards. Having tested two MB-1s, the US Navy ordered ten similar machines, with provision for torpedo-dropping and designated TM-1. Later, following experience in the quantity-production of the Curtiss types just mentioned, Martin designed an improved version called the T3M-1. An entirely new fuselage, of welded steel construction, was a feature, and further development and production involved the Great Lakes Aircraft Corporation.

In 1925 an order was placed by the US Navy for three big Boeing TB-1 torpedo-droppers. Though these were the sole examples delivered, they were in service for several years. Vastly greater and more enduring success rewarded the work of Douglas, and in 1925 this company designed an entirely new twin-engined torpedo-dropping biplane, quite comparable in many ways with the much later and

◀ The Grumman Avenger, also known as the TBF and TBM, was the US Navy's standard torpedo-bomber of the Second World War. Nearly 10,000 Avengers were built and they also served with the Royal Navy and the Royal New Zealand Air Force.

larger German Heinkel He 59. It has already been stated that the de Havilland Sea Mosquito was the first twin-engined torpedo-dropper to land aboard an aircraft-carrier (March 1944); but there is some evidence that a Douglas XT2D-1 was 'operated off' the USS *Langley*. The designation given was one of several applied to aircraft of the Douglas type now under general consideration, and which served as shore-based patrol aircraft until 1937.

The chief claim to distinction by the Douglas TBD, later named Devastator, was that it was the first monoplane to be ordered for service from aircraft-carriers of the US Navy. Biplanes with large wing area had hitherto been preferred because the relatively low loading per square foot of area (wing loading) gave them docile handling qualities for operation from the confines of a carrier's deck, allied with low speeds at landing and take-off. They were thus more forgiving to minor indiscretions in airmanship; and pilots still tended to look upon the monoplane as being 'hotter' to handle generally, being prone, for example, to drop a wing (in the sense of dipping sideways) on approaching to land. Some of their notions were purely imaginary, though others were only too well founded. In any case, the monoplane form was bound to come for the torpedo-dropper as for every other major class of combat aeroplane, if only to maintain its

performance in closer approximation to that of contemporary fighters; and the first of the new Douglases, the XTB-1 (X for experimental) was very obviously superior to a Great Lakes biplane built to meet similar requirements, and likewise designed to operate from a new generation of carriers of which the USS *Ranger* was the first.

The XTB-1 was delivered to the US Navy in April 1935, and with its clean-cut, well-proportioned appearance, with long streamlined 'greenhouse', or transparent cockpit canopy, housing the crew of three in tandem, was clearly a trend-setter in its class. To name but one other innovation in a machine of this category, the mainwheels were retractable; they folded to the rear, and segments of them were left exposed (as on the historic Douglas DC airliners of the period), thus affording some protection in a belly landing, or with wheels inadvertently up. The 50 ft (15·2 m) wing span naturally demanded quite drastic reduction if any useful numbers of these monoplanes were to be housed in the hangars below the carrier's flight deck, or on the deck itself, and the main panels of the wing were arranged to fold upwards, instead of rearwards as had formerly been usual. No longer was this operation performed by man-power, but by a special hydraulic system, which, even though it meant one more item to maintain in working order, came as a boon and a blessing to those at work on the windswept deck. A Pratt & Whitney 800 hp engine gave a speed slightly above 200 mph (320 km/h), thus setting another entirely new standard and encouraging the Navy to order 129 production examples having various improvements, prominent among which was a raised canopy for the pilot.

When the Japanese attacks in the Pacific began late in 1941, about a hundred of these Douglases remained in service, and, now bearing their new name Devastator, went into action during February 1942 in the areas of the Marshall and Gilbert Islands. Fortunately opposition was then light, because defensive armament was two machine-guns only. A number of ships, including a cruiser, were claimed among their victims. Sadly, a heavy debit side to the account was to be rendered a few months later at the Battle of Midway, when, in a single day, no fewer than thirty-five of the sturdy Douglas monoplanes fell to anti-aircraft fire or pouncing Zero fighters. Like the RAF's Fairey Battles in France, they showed only too conclusively that heavy single-engined three-seaters could be terribly mauled by agile single-seaters.

A one-man crew was a notable feature of the Douglas torpedo-dropper which came next in the family line, and which, being smaller and more powerful than its predecessor, was very much faster, being capable of nearly 350 mph (560 km/h). This new type, the BTD-1, or Destroyer, was originally designed as a dive-bomber, and had anhedral angle on the inboard sections of the wing, a characteristic design and recognition feature of the German Junkers Ju 87, which will command a pre-eminent place in the chapter dealing with aircraft of the dive-bomber class. As a torpedo-dropper, however, the Destroyer never achieved distinction, and only twenty-eight were built. Nevertheless, it was a pointer towards the world-famous Douglas Skyraider, which, as this book is written, gives service in Vietnam with undiminished vigour as a dive-bomber and ground-attack aircraft. This is remarkable indeed, for the first Skyraider contracts were placed as long ago as July 1944.

Our present concern, however, is torpedo-dropping, and in this capacity the Skyraider achieved no fame in the Second World War, for it was not to enter service until 1947, and was, in any case, more urgently required for other duties, notably anti-submarine. Like all the other varied weapon-loads this willing war-horse was called upon to carry, the 'fish' was slung externally, whereas in the Destroyer it was snug inside the clean-lined fuselage. A less familiar counterpart of the Skyraider was the Martin AM-1 Mauler, and this was a name that was highly appropriate, if only by reason of

some startling publicity photographs which showed it carrying not only *three* torpedoes (one under the fuselage and one under each wing) but an impressive array of bombs in addition. With special emphasis on 'publicity' we may dismiss this big, handsome single-seater, for only about 150 were built and these saw little first-line service.

The name of Grumman was a much-respected one in the US Navy from the very early 1930s, especially in regard to fighters; but not until 1940 did this company receive an order for two experimental torpedo-droppers. The outcome was one of the most successful carrier-borne aircraft of all time, having the name Avenger, though known by many other numerical and alphabetical designations (including TBF and TBM) according to improvements incorporated or new-found tasks. In all of these designations, however, the letter T, signifying torpedo, came first in order, and as a torpedo-dropper the Avenger was something new. Defensive armament, for instance, was not omitted in favour of higher speed and all-round performance, as in the Destroyer, but was prominently proclaimed by a bulbous power-driven gun turret, housing a heavy machine-gun; this was additional to two lighter machine-guns, one in the ventral position, for downward fire, and one for the pilot. Three men formed the crew, and the one who aimed the bombs

when these were carried as an alternative load to the torpedo, was also called upon to man the ventral gun. The torpedo or 2,000 lb (907 kg) of bombs were both internal loads, for the Avenger's fuselage was spacious, and, like the Skyraider, it was pressed into service for duties never at first imagined. Numbered among these was its operation sometimes as a *seven*-seater, for 'Carrier On-board Delivery' duties, or ferrying supplies or personnel.

The Avenger's family descendant was the Guardian, and all that need be said of this aeroplane at present is that, in the experimental stage at least, defensive armament was entirely abandoned, giving place to a speed-augmenting jet engine in the tail, to assist the 2,600 hp piston engine in the nose. Even scantier reference is called for by the Vought Sea Wolf, for although having certain advantages over the Avenger, which it resembled, and although ordered for massive production, which was sharply stopped in September 1945, it never served with the squadrons.

Although of vastly greater importance than the Sea Wolf, the far bigger, twin-engined, shore-based Lockheed Neptune is yet one other US Navy type which calls for mention, for the reason that its internal load could be in the form of two torpedoes.

Following hard upon such terrifying names as Devastator, Destroyer, Skyraider and Mauler the

◀ Although the Douglas Skyraider has its rightful and primary place in this volume among the torpedo-droppers it has been far more extensively employed in recent years for dive-bombing. This late example carries a fuel tank under the fuselage and bombs beneath the wings.

already familiar appellation Cuckoo must seem a little whimsical; but there was nothing whimsical about an order for six of these carrier-borne torpedo-droppers placed by the Japanese Navy with a British air mission during 1921. Yet though design thereafter was predominantly in the hands of Japanese constructors, the influence of British techniques and skills was not to disappear for several years to come.

The greatest Japanese companies associated with the class of aircraft under review were Mitsubishi and Nakajima, and to the former company's products we must now turn, for the first of these, known for short as 1MTs, was not only the first torpedo-dropper to be built in Japan, but was designed by Herbert Smith, formerly of the Sopwith company. The most remarkable feature of this aeroplane was its triplane wing structure, as favoured by Sopwith for several types of fighters and bombers; and British influence extended even further, for the first test flight was made, in August 1922, by a Capt Jordan. Twenty 1MTs were built, and, in common with the Cuckoo, Swift and Dart, they carried no guns in addition to the torpedo, either for attack or defence.

The next of the Mitsubishi torpedo-droppers was likewise built to Herbert Smith's designs; but this was a biplane, and, although the first example was completed as early as January 1923, in developed form the type saw service with the Japanese aircraft-carrier force until 1938. This service was very extensive, and a point of particular interest is that a B1M, as the type was known, became the first Japanese military aircraft to be engaged in air combat, for in February 1933 three of these machines, escorted by the same number of fighters, jointly destroyed an American-built and American-flown Chinese Air Force Boeing P-12 fighter near Shanghai.

Next in line came the B2M, which was yet another type embroiled in the 'Shanghai Incident', but one designed and built by the British Blackburn company, and first delivered, in specimen form, during 1930. This held the additional distinction of being the first Japanese-operated machine of its class to have a metal-framed structure, and, although it had several superficial points in common with the Ripon, it was distinguished by two pairs of struts between the wings on each side, instead of a single pair, thus making it a biplane of two-bay, and not single-bay form. One Blackburn designation was, in fact, 'Ripon (Hispano-Suiza)', denoting not only its kinship with the British-operated Ripon, but its French engine also.

As the 1930s advanced, the time arrived to consider abandoning biplanes altogether, and the Mitsubishi B5M1, which entered production in 1937, was a very clean-lined three-seater, somewhat in the style of the Devastator, though having Spitfire-like (semi-elliptical) wings but a fixed under-carriage. The production run was a short one, leaving Mitsubishi free to concentrate on military types of other classes.

Respecting Mitsubishi, in fact, it remains only to mention the Ki-67 Hiryu (Flying Dragon), which, as recorded in the companion volume dealing with bombers (for to this class it truly belonged), was essentially an Army, and not a Navy, type. In spite of this, it was engaged in the Battle of the Philippine Sea as a torpedo-dropper also, though manned by Army crews under Naval direction.

The Nakajima company began the design and construction of torpedo-droppers much later than Mitsubishi, but with a resoundingly successful type, which, in its own way, came as a surprise almost as

In the Nakajima B5N the Imperial Japanese Navy possessed one of the finest and most successful torpedo-droppers ever built. For such an aircraft the Allied code-name Kate seemed a trifle plain.

unpleasant to its US and British opponents in the Second World War as did the Mitsubishi Zero fighter. Though having the Japanese designation B5N, the new Nakajima, a monoplane of strikingly handsome appearance, was eventually given the Allied code-name Kate; and any Shakespeare-student may be assured that the kiss of this particular Kate was indeed the kiss of death, for though somewhat resembling in essentials the US Navy's Devastator, it was of later design, and of higher all-round effectiveness, and embodied, for example, a fully retractable undercarriage. Though at first employed for bombing, its alternative load was a single 1,765 lb (800 kg) torpedo, and the suspension of this weapon under the fuselage presented no difficulty because the bombs were attached in a line, one behind the other, just as on British seaplanes of the First World War. This simplified the designer's ever-demanding task of locating the centre of gravity, for in terms of weight distribution there is little difference between a string of bombs and a torpedo some 16 ft (5 m) long, or about half the length of the aeroplane itself.

The effectiveness of this alternative armament was grimly demonstrated in the assault on the US Fleet at Pearl Harbor, when 103 machines of this general type, carrying bombs, delivered their strike in partnership with forty similar torpedo-droppers.

Although capable of carrying a torpedo, the Japanese Nakajima C6N Saiun (Painted Cloud)was so fast – having such cleanness of line as this picture bears witness – that it was mainly employed for reconnaissance and fighting.

At least half that number of torpedoes found their mark on battleships, which included the *Arizona* and *Oklahoma*, and in the months to follow, the deadly Nakajimas delivered fatal blows against the United States aircraft-carriers *Lexington*, *Yorktown* and *Hornet*.

As Kate grew too elderly for first-line service, another extremely fine Nakajima type, the B6N

Tenzan (Heavenly Mountain), became increasingly in evidence, being first encountered in December 1943 during an attack by a US task force on the Marshall Islands. Though strongly resembling its predecessor, it was very much faster, having a top speed of just under 300 mph (480 km/h), whereas Kate, in her time, had done well to exceed 200 mph (320 km/h). Yet even this improved performance seemed sluggish when compared with that attained by the C6N Saiun (Painted Cloud), one of the most graceful aeroplanes ever built, and capable of nearly 380 mph (610 km/h), though without a torpedo in place. So fast, indeed, was the Saiun that it was used mainly for reconnaissance and fighting.

Although Japan had lost all her aircraft-carriers by the time it arrived in service, brief reference must be made to the Aichi B7A Ryusei (Shooting Star), which resembled the Douglas Destroyer in having a 'cranked', or 'inverted-gull', wing but carried a defensive gunner. Operating from shore bases, this fine machine was used for suicide attacks, or strikes, as were several other types of Japanese aircraft. This means that they were deliberately flown into their targets in order not to miss – a technique proposed by an Englishman well before the 1914 war but never before exploited with such terrible effect.

Certainly among the most astonishing aircraft of all time, and one that was absolutely unique, was the Aichi M6A Seiran (Mountain Haze), a seaplane which could carry a torpedo or a bomb load and which could drop not only these weapons but its floats as well, so that on returning from a mission the pilot would 'ditch' and be rescued – by the submarine from which his Seiran had been launched! Among the missions planned for these aircraft, but never effected, was the blocking of the Panama Canal.

Although torpedoes could be dropped by the big four-engined Kawanishi flying-boats these are not appropriate for consideration here; and with two Yokosuka types, one early and one late, this account of Japanese torpedo-droppers must close. The early one was the B4Y carrier-borne biplane of the mid-1930s, and which served until 1940; the late one was the twin-engined land-based P1Y Ginga (Milky Way), which was primarily a bomber but could also number the torpedo among its possible weapon loads.

This present narrative now having spanned the Pacific, attention must be transferred across the Asian continent, though the Russian contribution will be relatively brief. One reason for this is that the Soviet Union never possessed an aircraft-carrier, and, although a seaplane version of the great Sikorsky Il'ya Muromets was flown before war came in 1914, there is no record of any such aircraft having been used as torpedo-droppers. It was not, in fact, until the early stages of the second world conflict that any type worthy of serious consideration was developed, and this was a straightforward modification of the Ilyushin DB-3F twin-engined landplane bomber. Its single torpedo was carried externally, and weighed over 2,000 lb (907 kg). There were, it is true, seaplane versions of big Russian monoplane bombers built between the wars and bearing the eminent name of Tupolev, but if a torpedo was numbered among their weapons its employment was of minor importance. Yet the same great name can be associated with what appears to have been the world's first jet-propelled torpedo-dropper, namely the Tu-14, which entered service on a limited scale in about 1950 and could carry two torpedoes as an alternative load to bombs.

From Russia we must now look to France, and go back from the 1950s to 1909, for it was in that year that Clément Ader, one of the most renowned, yet controversial, figures in the entire history of flight published a treatise which mentioned not only aircraft-carriers much in the form in which they are known today, but torpedo-dropping aircraft to operate from them.

The earliest French twin-engined torpedo-droppers were in the Farman F.160/168 range, developed from the gawky, angular Goliath airliners that were so familiar to European air travellers in the 1920s. The Goliath itself was originally a converted bomber, but in respect of torpedo-dropping it must be recorded that no fewer than four examples in the range of Goliath-developments bore the official French class designation 'Torp 4', signifying that they were four-seaters using the torpedo as their primary weapon. For many years big seaplanes of this family served with the Aéronautique Maritime.

The second association with airliners is a more striking one still, entailing as it did the conversion of the famous Latécoère 28 high-wing monoplanes from mail- or passenger-carrying to torpedo-dropping. By coincidence the Latécoère airliners carried eight passengers, recalling the 'Carrier On-board Delivery' development of the American Douglas Skyraider, a type designed with torpedo-dropping as a dominant requirement! Such is the adaptability of basically well-designed load-carrying aeroplanes, and such were the high-wing Latécoères, as represented here by the Type 290.

From the high-wing monoplane formula the Latécoère concern next turned, for their Type 298 torpedo-dropper, to what has more than once been described as a low-wing layout, though this is strictly incorrect, for the wing was sufficiently far above the bottom of the fuselage for internal torpedo-stowage. The Latécoère 298 was one of the finest-looking single-engined seaplanes ever built, and dated from 1936. A fact that is, perhaps, too little known is that, although French Naval seaplanes of this type were never to launch torpedoes in action, they served as bombers side by side with landplanes of the French Air Force in attempting to stem the German advance on the Somme in 1940.

What has been said concerning the appearance of the Latécoère 298 would certainly not hold true of the much earlier Lioré et Olivier and Levasseur biplane torpedo-droppers of the 1920s and 1930s. The latter company (the name of which must not be confused with that of the famous French pioneer designer Leon Levavasseur, who was responsible for the historic Antoinette monoplane), was nevertheless astute enough to acquire a licence to build British Blackburn torpedo-droppers, and the first design of its own greatly resembled the Dart. The company's later two/three-seater seaplanes (PL 14 and PL 15) were equivalent to, though quite different from, the Ripon.

A story of uncommon interest remains to be told concerning the last of the French types to be reviewed, namely the Bloch 175 twin-engined monoplane. Only a small number of these bombers had been completed by the time of the Franco-German Armistice in 1940, but though the Germans recognised their excellent qualities and authorised construction of more, these were unarmed, and engines intended for yet others were transferred to the huge Messerschmitt Me 323 transports. Production of the Bloch 175 ceased in 1942, but shortly after the war was over the French Navy expressed a need for new torpedo-droppers – and so back into production went the erstwhile bomber, now designated 175T.

Thus the type was more or less contemporary with, as well as being comparable with, the Bristol Brigand, though this, as already recounted, was a torpedo-dropper turned bomber!

To honour the Dutch nation as a once-great maritime power, and equally to acclaim the name

The Fokker T.IV was a twin-float, twin-engined seaplane torpedo-dropper, like the German Heinkel He 115, but was of earlier design and distinctly less elegant.

of Fokker – familiar as producer of fighters, bombers and airliners – we may bring this survey of torpedo-dropping aircraft towards its conclusion by recording that, in 1927, the Fokker company constructed the first of a number of twin-engined seaplanes known by the type-number T.IV. A full eight years later this same type of torpedo-dropper was ordered back into production, thus echoing the story of the Bloch 175. A later, smaller and handier type was the T.VIII-W, a few of which were pressed into service with RAF Coastal Command, though not in their intended rôle of torpedo-droppers.

	Span		Length		Crew	Loaded weight	Maximum speed	Armament
USA								
Douglas DT-2	50′	0″	37′	8″	2	7,293 lb	99 mph	1 torp+1 m-g
Douglas Devastator	50′	0″	35′	0″	3	10,194 lb	206 mph	1 torp or bombs+2 m-g
Grumman Avenger	54′	2″	40′	0″	3	15,904 lb	270 mph	1 torp or bombs+3 m-g
JAPAN								
Nakajima B5N	50′	11″	33′	11″	3	8,050 lb	217 mph	1 torp or bombs+2 m-g
FRANCE								
Latécoère 298	50′	10″	41′	2″	2–3	10,095 lb	180 mph	1 torp or bombs+3 m-g
Bloch 175T	58′	11″	41′	5″	3	18,740 lb	323 mph	1 torp or bombs+4 m-g

torp=torpedo   m-g=machine-gun

4

Attack and Assault

The two words that comprise the heading of this chapter are, of course, synonymous; yet they convey with force the essence of the chapter's contents, which is the development of a class of aeroplane designed specifically for low-flying offensive work against ground targets, with mobile military ones particularly in mind, and issued to specially trained squadrons. To the US Army Air Service (as the USAF then was) the machines concerned were known as attack airplanes, or more colloquially, attack ships; while to the Italians, who alone among other nations exploited the same idea, the term *assalto* had the same significance.

An acquaintanceship with this class of aeroplanes is best effected by renewing that already established with the Junkers J.I. In pursuing a similar line of development the Americans decided soon after the 1914–18 war to go one better – and this was literally so, for the aircraft concerned was not a biplane but a triplane. Certainly it needed all the wing area possible to lift its specified load of armour and armament; and the resulting monstrosity – a carefully chosen description – was not only sluggish on the controls but woefully slow, having an all-out speed of about 100 mph (160 km/h).

Experience over the years had already shown that speed was a desirable asset in strike aircraft of any form, always assuming, of course, that this could be reconciled with the accurate delivery of weapons; yet the scantiest attention was given to this consideration when planning the Boeing (Engineering Division) GA-1, initially known as the GA-X, or Ground Attack Experimental, and built in 1920 at McCook Field. The triplane wings spanned over 65 ft (nearly 20 m), and were heavily braced by strut-assemblies of N formation, a precautionary measure against concentrated return fire, while $\frac{1}{4}$-in (6·3 mm) armour plating, totalling about a ton in weight, protected the crew and the two 435 hp Liberty water-cooled engines. These engines drove pusher propellers, and were mounted on the middle wing. Jointly with the abundant area of the three wings, the power was sufficient to lift not only the load mentioned but a 37 mm cannon in the nose, and a machine-gun in the same position – both in charge of one gunner; a rear position, with one machine-gun firing upwards and two downwards, again manned by a single gunner; and – just to complete this fantastic concept of a 'giant battle-plane', as envisioned in boys' books of earlier years – a gunner in the front of each engine housing, both men wielding twin machine-guns!

The now-famous name of Boeing came into the designation because this company won a contract to build twenty such aeroplanes, but tests in Mexico were so disappointing that the order was halved, and the GA-1 became extinct, like the dinosaur it resembled in so many ways. As Peter M. Bowers recalled amusingly in his book *Boeing Aircraft since 1916* 'The GA-1s were grossly overweight because of their armour, crew visibility was poor, and there were serious aerodynamic and cooling problems.

'In spite of these deficiencies all ten were accepted by the Army and delivered by rail to Kelly Field,

Texas, where their poor characteristics endowed them with a unique disciplinary function. All a commander had to do to keep exuberant young pilots on their best behaviour was to threaten to assign them to the triplanes.'

As rational in design as the GA-1 was exotic, was the British de Havilland D.H.4 single-engined two-seater, variants of which were built in the USA not only in great quantities, but in bewildering pro-fusion in terms of adaptation, remaining in service until 1928 for attack, as well as reconnaissance duties.

Although there were several experimental 'attack ships' in the 1920s, some of them almost as remark-able in their own ways as was the GA-1, later development followed more closely along D.H.4 lines; or, in terms of what has been related con-cerning the First World War, the handy Hannover CL, rather than the ponderous Junkers J.I, was the true historical precedent. Not until 1926, however, did the US Army Air Service formally restate its requirements for new attack aircraft, and both the Douglas and Curtiss companies advanced proposals. The outcome was the adoption, as standard equip-ment for attack squadrons, of the Curtiss A-3, a two-seat biplane of notably clean and neat appear-ance, stemming largely from its makers' close associations with racers and fighters. The pilot had

A heavy machine-gun armament and relatively light bomb load were characteristics of the Curtiss A-3B 'attack' biplane. ▶

two fixed forward-firing machine-guns, and the gunner another pair. These rear guns were on a mounting of the famous, and almost universally adopted, British Scarff ring-type. Light bombs, commonly of the 'fragmentation' type, for use against troops, were carried under the wings.

Inevitably, as in other classes of military and civil aircraft which came into being during the 1930s, the monoplane form made a strong appeal to the Curtiss designers working on a projected replacement for the A-3, and this form they adopted with the particular intention of obtaining higher speeds. The aeroplane which resulted was to become familiar as the A-8 Shrike, and an order for a 'Service test' batch (this status being denoted by affixing the letter Y before the A), was placed in September 1931.

There were several unusual features about this new aeroplane. First, the monoplane wing was not a thick one, as was common at the time (either without any external bracing whatever or braced by rigid struts), but a thin one instead, and braced by wires. True, there were two struts on each side, in the form of an inverted V, but these merely ran from the fuselage to the attachment points for the undercarriage; and it was this undercarriage which was another of the unusual features, for, being fixed and not retractable, it was streamlined by quite

immense casings, or fairings. The size of these fairings was not entirely due to the wheels and their associated shock-absorbers, for they housed in addition two of the four fixed, forward-firing machine-guns, the other pair being mounted in the wings. The gunner, who had a protective hood, as had the pilot (representing another innovation of the period), had a fifth machine-gun on what the Americans termed a 'flexible' mounting, meaning simply that the gun it carried was movable. A typical additional offensive load was four 100-lb (45 kg) bombs.

A later version of this same aeroplane, the A-12, had a Wright Cyclone air-cooled engine in place of the former Curtiss Conqueror liquid-cooled type, this being less vulnerable to return fire from the ground, and also lighter; but the name Shrike was common to both versions.

The naming of American military aircraft was, at the time, unusual. With its menacing appearance, accentuated by its huge wheel fairings, and with the howl of its Conqueror or Cyclone engine, the Shrike was an impressive aeroplane, especially as it streaked low to rake its target with gunfire and release its bombs to shatter or scatter its target. A 'Shrike strike', as it would be known today, must have been a shattering experience.

Somewhat perversely, it seems, and certainly con-

The Curtiss A-12 Shrike.

fusingly, the name Shrike was also conferred upon a new Curtiss attack machine which was, in fact, a totally new design, being, in the first place, twin-engined. Its official designation was A-18, and it afforded its pilot and gunner the possibility of getting home if one engine was put out of action – a comforting consideration in a hazardous occupation, but one which had not applied to the old GA-1, for this had to work very hard indeed to sustain its great weight in the air even with both engines working.

The new Shrike dated from the mid-1930s, but

was never built in appreciable numbers, for US policy thereafter favoured what was known at the time as the 'attack bomber', the accent being on the latter word, as signifying the dominant weapon carried. From this new policy grew aeroplanes of a general type which were eventually to bear such illustrious names as Boston, Mitchell, Maryland, Baltimore, and Invader; but these will be dealt with later. Meanwhile only one remaining American attack machine demands consideration. This was a product of the Northrop Corporation, and was related to their Gamma and Delta civil monoplanes which rivalled in speed their Lockheed counterparts.

To allude to this Northrop type as one machine is permissible though not meticulously true, for there were two principal versions, the A-17 with fixed undercarriage (far less obtrusive than the Shrike's, because all four of the pilot's machine-guns were in the low monoplane wing), and the A-17A, with retractable 'gear', to use American terminology. These fine Northrops began to come into service in the summer of 1935, but although they were built in sufficient quantities to equip several 'attack groups', their active life and further development were curtailed by the change in policy already noted.

Fixed undercarriages on monoplanes have as

Light fragmentation bombs, for use against troops, are seen being loaded aboard a Northrop A-17A monoplane before a low-flying attack sortie during manoeuvres in the late 1930s.

prominent a place in this chapter as they had on the aeroplanes themselves, and the first of the Italian *assalto* types, the Caproni A.P.1, was yet another type displaying this characteristic. It first appeared in 1934, but sufficient numbers were built to equip only one *Stormo d'Assalto* (the equivalent of an American attack group) and to export a few more. Nothing further need be added, for good, sturdy aeroplane though it was, the A.P.1 had no particular distinction apart from being the first Italian machine of its class. More distinctive, however, was the generally comparable, but slightly later, Breda Ba 65, for not only was its undercarriage retractable but it was built entirely of metal, whereas the A.P.1 had much wood in its structure – a favourite Italian practice. No less significant, the gunner (when one was carried, for many Ba 65s were single-seaters) had a neat little power-driven turret for his machine-gun. This gun was of 12·7 mm calibre, or bore, as were two of the four guns fixed in the wings, the others being of 7·7 mm calibre. Bomb load, too, was heavier than on the A.P.1, consisting, for example, of two 800-lb (360 kg) bombs or 160 smaller ones for use against personnel.

The Breda company was thus encouraged to pro-

A formation of Regia Aeronautica Breda Ba 65s.

ceed with a totally new design, to which they gave the number Ba 88. With its two massive 1,000 hp engines, contrasting sharply with the small size of the wings and fuselage, it presented an impression of speed which was amply realised when, in December of 1937, the year in which the type first appeared, it established a number of international speed records for machines of its weight-carrying class, just as the Heinkel He 115 torpedo-dropper was soon to do in its own category. In full service trim the Ba 88 could (or so the makers claimed) attain about 300 mph (480 km/h), but it was tricky to handle and never popular with its pilots. Nevertheless, just over a hundred were built, and many of these served with the 7th Gruppo Autonomo Combattimento in Libya and in Corsica with the 19th Gruppo. But this was to be the last of the Italian types designed especially for 'assault', and attempts to develop it as a dive-bomber were unsuccessful.

The story of specialised attack machines ends with the most famous and successful representative of the class ever constructed. This is the Russian Stormovik, at one time known as the BSh-2 (the letters signifying Bronirovannii Shturmovik, or 'armoured attacker'), but more familiar as the Il-2, denoting the fact that the famous Sergei Vladimirovich Ilyushin was in charge of the design.

In applying the word 'successful' to this aeroplane

it is meant not merely in the technical sense but in the operational sense also; and the Stormovik came to mean to the Russian people what the Spitfire and Hurricane meant to the British, or the Ju 87 Stuka to the Germans. In other words, it became a national symbol, and if ever an aeroplane epitomised the iron will of a nation it was this.

The Russians had long appreciated the desirability of having armoured aircraft for low-flying attacks on any enemy forces which might assail its sprawling frontiers, though not, in particular, on tanks or other armoured vehicles. There was, for instance, an experimental armoured version of the I-16 fighter, having four machine-guns firing obliquely downwards, another pair in the wings for frontal fire, and two 110-lb (50 kg) bombs; but in 1935 priority was ordered for the development of a true 'tank-killer', suitable, in fact, for attacking any strongpoint, mobile or otherwise, and in face of fierce opposing fire.

Several designs were studied, and one twin-engined type having no fewer than four 37-mm cannon, as well as a defensive machine-gun, was brought to the stage of testing; but so great was the recoil of the immense armament – for such it was at the time – that the pilot's aim was hopelessly impaired, and meanwhile the problem of building quickly and in numbers a suitable aircraft to meet

the possible threat of German armoured power became ever more pressing.

Against strong competition from the designer Sukhoi – a name which is today world-famous respecting strike aircraft in particular – Ilyushin finally produced a prototype which seemed to meet the demands, and this was tested in late 1940 and early 1941. Now bearing its familiar designation Il-2, the new attacker was ordered into instant production, and just when the first few examples had been completed Germany invaded Russia. So urgent was the demand that the Il-2s were sent forthwith into action, and such was their success that the constructors are said to have received from Stalin himself a telegram which read: 'The Red Army needs the Il-2 as much as it needs bread.'

At this time the Il-2 was a single-seater, and losses caused by enemy fighters were so heavy that early in 1942 the decision was taken to develop a two-seat version having a gunner for defence. But this additional armament was of secondary importance to the offensive power at the command of the Il-2's pilot, and novel among his weapons (which could include various combinations of guns and bombs) were rocket projectiles, or what the RAF later came to know as RPs, by which contraction they will hereafter be noted in the data tables.

A point about the RP that is sometimes over-

Heavily armoured and thick-winged though it was, the Russian Ilyushin Il-2 Stormovik could not justly be dubbed a 'furniture van', like its forerunner the Junkers J.1 of the First World War.

looked, because of the weapon's great destructive power, especially in penetrating armour, is that there is no recoil, as with a big gun; and they were, furthermore, simple in form and easy to make in the quantities in which the Il-2s used them up.

The aeroplane itself was also a straightforward one, in spite of its unusual features. The low-set monoplane wing was very thick in section and was of all-metal construction, whereas the fuselage was a composite structure, the forward part being of metal and the rear part of wood. The main wheels of the undercarriage retracted rearwards into blister-like fairings, which, nevertheless, left part of each wheel exposed. The single engine was a twelve-cylinder liquid-cooled AM-38 of 1,300 hp, and behind it, under a short canopy, sat the pilot and gunner. But this was no ordinary canopy, for it was protected extensively by armour-plate and armoured glass; and this was additional to a veritable shell of armour-plate enclosing the engine, radiator, oil-cooler, fuel tanks and those portions of the crew's anatomies that were not screened by the canopy.

The total weight of this protection was over 1,500 lb (680 kg), representing fifteen per cent or more of the entire loaded weight of the aircraft.

Set in the wings were two 20-mm cannon and two 7·6-mm machine-guns, the barrels of the cannon projecting well forward of the leading edge outboard of the undercarriage. The gunner had a 12·7-mm machine-gun, a useful weapon not only against interfering fighters, but ground targets also, especially after the pilot had delivered the main strike load. Under the wings were attachment points for guide rails, and on to these rails the eight RPs, weighing 56 lb (25 kg) each, were slid. If bombs were carried instead of the RPs, these were stowed in four cells, located inboard of the undercarriage.

Remarkably enough, the Il-2s had numerous successes against enemy aircraft as well as tanks, and the newspaper *Krasnyi Flot (Red Fleet)* reported: 'The Il-2's firepower, invulnerability and manoeuvrability have been proved many times. In arduous combat conditions our best assault pilots have frequently been on the winning side in duels with German aircraft.'

The German aircraft concerned were not infrequently Junkers Ju 87 dive-bombers, but before dealing with these, and other machines of their class the fact must be recorded that an improved and more powerful version of the Il-2, known as the Il-10, began to reach Soviet ground-attack units late in 1944, and was soon in action – not over its homeland, which the Il-2 had done so much to save, but over the enemy's own territory.

In Germany there had originated in 1939 the Henschel Hs 129, a type of aircraft which is strictly comparable with the Il-2 in being heavily armoured in the forward section and round the pilot's cockpit, for it was a single-seater although it had two engines. These engines were at first of German Argus type, and performance was poor because the total power delivered was under 1,000 hp, and less than that available to typical single-seat fighters of the period, such as the Hurricane, for example, which was itself to be used as an anti-tank aircraft as was the Henschel Hs 129. Under this designation development of the new German machine proceeded, despite its many shortcomings, but with the fall of France good quantities of Gnome-Rhône engines, having the more useful output of nearly 700 hp each, became available, and these were duly installed in production-type Hs 129s. It was, in fact, much the same story as has already been related concerning the Bloch 175 and the Messerschmitt Me 323, and thus freshly powered the new German type became far more battleworthy and saw its first action during the Crimean campaign of 1942.

The Hs 129 served also in North Africa, and the

◀ One weak spot of the Il-2 was its lack of rear defence, a deficiency largely remedied by installing a gunner. In formation, as seen, the later two-seaters gave mutually defensive fire.

present writer, in his capacity as an RAF technical intelligence officer, received from colleagues there (among other sources) sufficient particulars to compile a detailed report on its features and capabilities. Having learned that specimens had already been examined by the Russians, he requested certain information (having previously provided them with a copy of his own report) in the expectation that the version or versions encountered by Britain's Allies might differ in certain respects from that he had already described in the report. A signal eventually arrived from Russia, and after due processing and deciphering turned out to be a truly excellent account of the new German aeroplane – as, indeed, it might well have been, for it was all his own original report! But doubtless the Russians were far too busy shooting-up German tanks and shooting down German aeroplanes to pay much regard to the finer points of technical intelligence, and in any case the Hs 129 appeared in several versions.

A representative armament on the Hs 129 was two 20-mm cannon and two 7·9-mm machine-guns, plus a 30-mm cannon with thirty shells. This big gun was alternative to a bomb load; but even this armament was unimaginative compared with such experimental installations as rocket projectiles, a flame-thrower and a battery of vertically-mounted mortars, each loaded with a 77-mm shell and trig-

A few examples of the Henschel Hs 129 were fitted with a 75-mm cannon, as shown, and could knock out a Joseph Stalin tank with one hit. Other armament was reduced, but marked unwieldiness resulted.

gered-off by a photo-electric cell actuated by the magnetic field created by a tank.

Such experiments were among the multitude of German 'might-have-beens', and production of the Hs 129 ended in the summer of 1944 after fewer than 900 had been built.

Interesting though it was, this aeroplane was never to be numbered among the truly great – as was the Stormovik.

	Span		Length		Crew	Loaded weight	Maximum speed	Armament
USA								
Curtiss A-3	38′	0″	28′	4″	2	4,378 lb	141 mph	4 m-g+bombs
Curtiss Shrike (A-12)	44′	0″	32′	3″	2	5,900 lb	177 mph	5 m-g+bombs
Northrop A-17A	47′	9″	31′	8″	2	7,550 lb	220 mph	5 m-g+bombs
ITALY								
Caproni A.P.1	39′	4″	28′	6″	2	4,916 lb	220 mph	3 m-g+bombs
Breda Ba 65	39′	8″	31′	6″	2	6,504 lb	225 mph	5 m-g+bombs
USSR								
Ilyushin Il-2	47′	11″	38′	3″	2	11,680 lb	270 mph	2 cannon+2 m-g+ bombs or RPs
GERMANY								
Henschel Hs 129	46′	7″	32′	0″	1	11,265 lb	253 mph	2 cannon+2 m-g+ bombs or one larger cannon

m-g=machine gun   RP=rocket projectile

5

Helldivers and Stukas

Because it has always made good sense to fly fast when flying low in the face of opposing fire, some of the earliest bomb-dropping aeroplanes – too early in time to be dignified with the name of 'bomber' – released their projectiles in a shallow dive to gain more speed, and sometimes to allow the pilot to see his target more clearly, for there were no proper sighting arrangements. This procedure is not to be confused with what was sometimes called glide-bombing, mainly practised at night to permit a silent, engine-off, approach to the target area. However, it can be closely related to the time when fighters began to be used for low attacks on ground targets, carrying small bombs to supplement their normal armament of fixed, forward-firing machine-guns. The use of these guns, in any case, entailed the pointing of the aircraft directly at the target, and as the pilots often dropped their bombs on the same 'pass' or 'run' during which they fired their guns, release was frequently not in level flight. On the contrary, the early ground-attack pilots were much preoccupied in hugging the contours of the ground, dodging round buildings and trees, ducking into valleys, and generally making themselves scarce – when they were not engaged, that is, in making sharp, steep turns and zooms. The zoom, or sudden climb under the impetus of gravity and engine power, was often a preliminary to a diving attack.

These aeroplanes were not dive-bombers in the sense that this very specialised form of aircraft will be examined in this chapter. The first machines to merit this distinction are difficult to identify, for it cannot be stated positively when pilots began to appreciate the deadly accuracy obtainable by diving at a steep and carefully calculated angle and pulling-

◄ The probably unsurpassable name of Helldiver was transferred to the Curtiss SBC biplane of the late 1930s. The wheels retracted into the fuselage sides.

out of the dive to allow for the 'lag' or 'trail' of the bombs on their way down to the target. However, a British Sopwith Camel single-seat fighter from the experimental station at Orfordness in Suffolk was being used as early as 1917 by Major Oliver Stewart, RFC, for scientific investigations into the potential of the new form of bombing attack.

Before this method could be put to practical and effective use in action, especially in delivering the heavier types of bomb, the First World War had ended, and only in the late 1920s and early 1930s did it become prominent in military and public attention. Some experts still contend that the Americans invented dive-bombing during this period but that it remained for the Germans to exploit it fully in the Second World War. Yet although this was not strictly the case, it was certainly the Americans, and in particular the US Navy, who made the greatest contributions to the practice and perfection of dive-bombing techniques. An early, official American definition of the actual term 'dive-bomber' described 'an aeroplane especially designed and equipped to carry out dive-bombing attacks', adding that it 'must be built so as to pull out of a steep dive, if necessary, with its bomb or bombs still attached, without breaking apart'.

In the context of the important proviso 'without breaking apart', and before relating the story of dive-bomber development in chronological sequence, it is instructive, and amusing, to quote a little-known statement by the German Junkers company soon after introducing their famous Ju 87 Stuka in later years. In a comment on the special speed-reducing air-brakes which were a feature of this aeroplane, Junkers emphasised: 'This means for limitation is not incorporated as a protection against structural failure, as requisite possibly in other designs of dive-bomber, but solely in thorough appreciation of tactical requirements for effective employment .... The brake makes it possible to approach the target closely without the crew experiencing excessive acceleration when levelling out and suffering deterioration in aiming. The aircraft can be pulled out of the fastest dive with full load and with diving-brake off in perfect safety.'

The amusement implicit in these German observations is to be gained by reflecting on just which 'other designs of dive-bomber' were in the writer's mind, for certainly the contemporary American types were designed to very stringent safety requirements, as the Germans well knew, and, as will later be seen, there were few others to consider.

Yet in these American and German statements there are points of special interest. First there was the emphasis on strength, a factor which was to become a dominant consideration not only in dive-bombers, but in much later forms of strike aircraft, typified by the Blackburn Buccaneer, which had to fly at extremely high speeds in turbulent air near the ground. The ability to pull out of a steep dive with a bomb load still in place was a convincing one, though such a contingency would be unlikely to arise on active service.

Then there is the Junkers reference to 'excessive acceleration', the latter word being technically designated as 'g', or gravity. It causes aircrew to black out, or become temporarily unconscious, during rapid changes of direction, the reason for this being the draining of blood from the brain. In such a circumstance deterioration of aim would certainly ensue. In the case of fighters, which flew at even higher speeds, the g-suit provided the answer; but the earlier types of dive-bomber were much slower, although dive-brakes, which presented added resistance to the air, came into general use with the faster monoplanes. In one experimental dive-bomber, an Italian Savoia Marchetti designed for the Germans, the pilot lay prone on his stomach, a posture which enabled him to accept higher g forces.

Although America's contribution to dive-bomber development was significant, the first and most famous American machine of this class to go into general service was not, strictly speaking, a dive-bomber at all, but was originally designated as a fighter. The story of this aeroplane may begin by recalling the film *Helldivers* of 1931–32. In this rip-roaring, heart-rending drama the stars were not only Clark Gable and Wallace Beery but some sturdy-looking two-seat Curtiss biplanes bearing the name of the film itself. To be exact, these renowned aeroplanes were essentially of the F8C type, the F signifying the primary duty of fighting. Like other types of US Naval and Marine fighters, most of which were single-seaters, the Helldiver was also very extensively used for the duty its name connoted, and, somewhat confusingly, this same name was retained for later, specialised dive-bombers of Curtiss design.

Especially memorable in the film were sequences depicting the Helldivers peeling off to enter their bombing dives from an echelon, or stepped-up, formation, the sharp sweepback on their upper wings accentuating their 'rarin' to go' appearance as they cartwheeled over in quick succession. One further note for film fans, which also serves to accentuate the physical appearance shared by US Navy single-seat fighters and the two-seat Helldiver, is that an old single-seat fighter Boeing was acquired by the stunt flyer and vintage-aircraft specialist Paul Mantz and remodelled to resemble a Curtiss Helldiver for a part in the film *Task Force* in the 1950s.

The original Helldiver was a development of the US Army Air Force's Falcon observation (reconnaissance) aircraft, but with a Pratt & Whitney Wasp air-cooled engine, as standardised by the Navy, instead of the liquid-cooled Curtiss D-12. Its full history is complicated, because although the two prototypes, ordered in 1927 and delivered in the following year, were nominated XF8C-1 (X for experimental) and were followed by F8C-1s and F8C-3s, the Marine Corps proceeded to redesignate them respectively as OC-1 and OC-3. Their bomb load was a light one – ten of 17 lb (7·7 kg); and they had two fixed forward-firing machine-guns and two similar guns free-mounted in the rear cockpit.

More formidable in attack was the XF8C-2, for this improved version could carry a single 500-lb (225 kg) bomb as an alternative to two bombs of 116 lb (52·6 kg). Next, in May 1930, came twenty-seven similar F8C4s, and some months later sixty-one F8C-5s, later redesignated O2C-1s. These were joined by another thirty for service with Marine and Navy units before final transference to Reserve squadrons.

Strikingly resembling the F8C Helldiver in over-all appearance, though of nearly 10 ft (3 m) greater span, and capable of delivering twice the load (a single bomb of 1,000 lb (450 kg)) in a diving attack, was the Martin BM-1 – the B indicating its function

of bomber. One other characteristic which stamped the BM-1 as a specialised bomber, as distinct from being dominantly a fighter, was the lighter armament of machine-guns – one fixed and one free. Only twelve BM-1s were built, but they were followed by twenty-one BM-2s. Prominent behind the engine, beneath the fuselage, were two parallel rods, called displacement arms. These were connected to the big bomb to swing it clear of the propeller on release at a steep diving angle, and thus prevent the bomber from bombing itself. This was said to have actually happened to a British Fairey Flycatcher, though the bombs concerned were small ones, and did not explode because they had not been made live. Displacement arms were thenceforth to become general fitments on specialised dive-bombers.

Comparable with the sturdy Martins were the Great Lakes BG-1s, sixty of which were built before the constructors' name faded from the aeronautical scene.

In 1936 two big new aircraft-carriers, the *Enterprise* and *Yorktown*, were launched for the US Navy, and at this period also that same service was displaying special interest in the SB (scout-bomber) class of aircraft, signifying that reconnaissance was a requirement equally with dive-bombing. To meet this need the Brewster company built an elegant-

The name Dauntless for the Douglas SBD, the most successful ▶
American dive-bomber of the Second World War, was
appropriate both in respect of its exploits and appearance.

looking mid-wing monoplane with a retractable undercarriage, the limited production of which (totalling only thirty) was entrusted to the Naval Aircraft Factory. Known as the SBN-1, this type was nevertheless interesting for two reasons: first, it represented a notable advance in performance over the somewhat earlier Vought SBU-1, a biplane with fixed undercarriage and greatly resembling a scaled-down Great Lakes BG-1; and secondly it was the forerunner of a more advanced design first flown in 1941 and officially styled SB2A. The US Navy named this aeroplane the Buccaneer, but the RAF called it the Bermuda and used it mainly as a target-tug, for it never saw first-line service. Comparable in being a monoplane in the same class, and also in having two names but no battle honours, was the Vought SB2U-1—Vindicator to the US Navy, Chesapeake to the Royal Navy.

The story of American dive-bombers, initiated by the original Helldiver, was far from being finished with such relatively insignificant types. Now the firms of Douglas and Curtiss entered the scene, and especially notable is the type-name Dauntless, by which one of the Douglas machines became world-famous. The official US Navy designation of this two-seat low-wing monoplane, which had a family relationship with the Northrop attack machines mentioned in the previous chapter, was SBD, but

the USAF did, in fact, order over six hundred which they knew as A-24s. In the history of air war, however, the Dauntless will always be remembered as the most successful carrier-borne dive-bomber ever built, for not only did it inflict some crippling casualties on the Japanese Fleet, notably in the battles of the Coral Sea, Midway and Solomons, but it was one of those aeroplanes which endeared itself to its crews for its ability to limp home in a hardly less crippled condition. As someone who knew the type remarked: 'She could take a frightful beating and stagger home on wings that sometimes looked like nutmeg graters.' This analogy was an appropriate one, for in a sense the wings resembled nutmeg graters even before the aeroplane went into action, because of the perforations in the flaps which formed the dive-brakes on the trailing edge of the wing. Displacement arms were fitted for a 1,000-lb (450 kg) or a 500-lb (225 kg) bomb under the fuselage, and beneath the wings were carriers for two bombs of 250 lb or 100 lb (113 or 45 kg). The pilot had two 0·5-in machine-guns immediately in front of him, and at the rear of the enclosure which housed the gunner also was a second pair, though these were of only 0·3-in calibre; otherwise their weight would have made them difficult to aim at high speed. With the resounding name of Helldiver this survey of American dive-bombers is concluded, for by that

Yet another Curtiss Helldiver – but differing essentially from its predecessors of the same name in being a monoplane, officially styled the SB2C.

same name went two very different and much later types than the film-famed original.

The first of this new pair of Helldivers – which together afforded an exceptionally interesting comparison in technical progress – represented more or less the ultimate in biplane design, having a very clean-lined fuselage, though one that was deep enough to house the retractable undercarriage, but still retaining a biplane wing structure. True, the wings themselves were more shapely, and were braced by only a single strut on each side; and, supplied to the US Navy as the SBC, the aeroplane was attractive enough for France to order a batch and for a few to be diverted to the RAF, these being known as Clevelands. Yet a Helldiver was never to distinguish itself in action, as did the dauntless Douglas; and this was equally true of the SBC's successor, the SB2C monoplane, although it was a very fine aeroplane, of which well over 7,000 were built. Some hundreds of these went to the USAF as A-25s, and hundreds more of the 7,000-odd were made in Canada.

If the Helldivers were never destined to be faded out in a flurry of glory, they at least won for themselves an honourable credit-line on the screen of aeronautical history; and they were still being cast by the US Navy in various rôles as late as 1949, just as they were some twenty years before.

Whether *Helldivers* was ever seen by Ernst Udet, fighter ace of the First World War, between-the-wars film stunt-pilot, and a founder-member and eminent leader of the re-created German Air Force, is unknown to the present writer; but beyond doubt Udet made a careful study of American dive-bombing techniques and found much joy, and doubtless instruction, in flying a Curtiss single-seat fighter/dive-bomber generally similar to the US Navy's F11C. To Udet more than to any other man, may be attributed the development and introduction into German service of a class of aeroplane called *Sturzkampfflugzeug*, shortened to Stuka and meaning dive-bomber. Of this class the Junkers

Ju 87 was incomparably the most famous example, and with this particular aeroplane the name Stuka has become generally identified.

Germany's first real attempt at making an aeroplane suitable for steep dive-bombing attacks as well as general military purposes was the Junkers K 47 of 1928, developed from a so-called 'mail-carrier' and likewise a low-wing monoplane of all-metal construction. External bracing gave additional stiffness to the wing to contend with sharp pull-outs, and the engine was a British Bristol Jupiter, just as the very first Ju 87 was to have a British Rolls-Royce Kestrel. The prototype of the K 47 was built in Sweden, and was used not only by the new German Air Force but by the Chinese. The sinister destiny of the type's descendant was never recognised when one K 47 was demonstrated in England at the Aerial Garden Party held at the Heston Air Park, near London, in July 1929. Eleven years were still to elapse before Ju 87s were fiercely engaged in actions over southern England; and they were years of progressive development.

Here Udet's name recurs, for it was his American-stimulated enthusiasm which rekindled a waning German interest, and which now led to the building and testing of experimental dive-bombers. Prominent among these was the Hamburger Ha 137, which, in having a cranked, or 'inverted-gull' wing

A single Junkers Ju 87 presented an unusually aggressive appearance, and this rare and intimate view of a large formation of these Stukas further accentuates the type's menacing aspect.

and a fixed, faired undercarriage, resembled not only a diminutive single-seat Ju 87, but also a somewhat disappointing British four-gun fighter to which the name Spitfire was unofficially applied, although this name was retained for a rather later eight-gun fighter, likewise a Supermarine product, which was by no means disappointing!

French dive-bombers, built in very small numbers, but also similar in general design to the Ha 137, were the Loire-Nieuport 40 and 41, though these had a rearward-retracting, and not a fixed, under-carriage. They were chiefly notable because one type of dive-brake tested was a split rudder, opening fan-fashion, while a second was simply the lowered undercarriage, fitted with big drag-producing shields.

The type of German dive-bomber selected for massive production was, as already intimated, the Ju 87, and this existed in many versions. It is here considered solely in its rôle of Stuka, and, notwithstanding early troubles, the deadly effectiveness of the type was made apparent in the later stages of the Spanish Civil War.

To remark that the Ju 87 was a frightening aeroplane is true in more senses than one. With its unusual wing form, stilty undercarriage, and sharply-sloping pointed nose to afford the pilot an unimpeded view for aiming his bombs, it was frightening in its mere physical appearance, although its air of sturdiness gave emphasis to the makers' claim that it was not prone to structural failure, or, as the Americans put it more vividly, to 'breaking apart'. Thus, the Ju 87 pilots and gunners were little concerned on this account, although they soon became acutely aware that the relatively low speed and light armament were grievous handicaps in combat, the same being the case with Britain's Fairey Battle, which was a near-equivalent, though it had no dive-brakes. For this reason the Stukas were provided with fighter escorts whenever possible; but, while it is true that Hurricane and Spitfire pilots may sometimes have felt like chuckling on placing a Ju 87 squarely in their gunsights it is equally true that nobody on the ground in a Stuka's bombing path would ever share the same emotion.

The bombing dive was commonly at an angle between about 70 degrees and the vertical, and the pull-out after release was abrupt and low, at a height of a few hundred feet. These facts alone were alarming enough, especially if anyone adjacent to the target had no cover to seek and could actually view the oncoming bomber at the final phase of its strike, for, like a skilfully handled fighter, a Stuka always attacked, when possible, out of the sun. The noise it made amplified the shock – the howl of the 1,200 hp Junkers Jumo 211 engine was sometimes augmented by 'screamers', or whistle-like attachments on the bombs, and even by a siren on one of the undercarriage legs, dubbed the 'Trombone of Jericho'. The bombs were carried beneath its fuselage and wings. The fuselage bomb was invariably a single and relatively heavy one, either of 1,000 lb (450 kg) if carried alone, or of 550 lb (250 kg) if forming part of a composite load with four bombs of 110 lb (50 kg), carried two under each wing, just outboard of the two fixed machine-guns provided for the pilot. The gunner had a single machine-gun, which was aimed by hand and gave scanty protection against fighters.

The Ju 87's dive-brakes, which were so vital to

The Ju 87 not only looked aggressive but made a frightening sound in a bombing dive. Seen instantly after release are a 550-lb bomb and four 110-pounders.

Best-known of all the Ju 87s were those of the B model, much improved compared with the A as used in Spain, and very extensively and effectively employed in the earlier campaigns of the war of 1939–45, not least in the Battle of Britain. To this version the foregoing description mainly applies, for it was the Ju 87B, together with the sub-type R (R standing for *Reichweite*, or range, signifying a bigger fuel supply), and the much-refined Ju 87D, with its single big bomb of 2,200 lb (1,000 kg) or even 3,000 lb (1,360 kg), which won for the Stuka an even more eminent place in history than the carrier-borne Douglas Dauntless. Little-known, perhaps, is the fact that a carrier-borne version of the Ju 87 itself was actually built, being intended for service with the German Navy's aircraft-carrier *Graf Zeppelin*, though this vessel was never completed and is not to be confused with the famous airship of the same name.

the aeroplane's successful functioning, were simple affairs: merely a pair of hinged slats under the wings, normally set edge-on to the airstream but turned through 90 degrees to offer maximum air-resistance and restrict the Stuka's speed in its headlong dive.

The importance of the dive-bomber in Germany's warlike plans, and the part played by Ernst Udet in the preparation of these, have already been made clear. The maiden flight of the first example of the Henschel Hs 123, the only other German dive-bomber to serve in the Second World War, was made by Udet himself. This type was a single-seat biplane with a fixed undercarriage, and like some of the first Ju 87s was tried under battle conditions

in Spain. Yet, even though the first flight had taken place in the spring of 1935, only a few months before that of the Ju 87, the Hs 123 was too primitive in concept, and was built in insufficient numbers, to achieve any great distinction in the war of 1939, whereas a second type of Henschel single-seat dive-bomber, the Hs 132, came too late. This, nevertheless, was far from being a mere 'paper project', such as the Germans drew up by the hundred, for prototype construction was already well advanced when the Russians overran the Henschel factory in 1945. The type is interesting for two particular reasons: first, the pilot lay prone; second, the single turbojet engine was mounted on top of the fuselage, just as on the little Heinkel Volksjäger fighter.

So strongly did the dive-bombing cult take hold in Germany during the late 1930s that the capability of making steep (though not near-vertical) diving attacks was demanded of large multi-engined bombers also – types that would alternatively, if not more normally, operate in level flight. The remarkable Ju 88, which has already been named as a torpedo-dropper, was fitted with dive-brakes that 'somewhat resembled farm gates', and for use in dive-bombing the pilot had a special sight, which could be swung aside when not in use in order not to obstruct his view.

For the generally comparable Dornier Do 217

two radically differing patterns of dive-brake were developed, the first, though unsuccessful, being particularly interesting, not merely because, when closed, it formed the rear extremity of the fuselage, but, even more remarkably, when opened out for a diving descent, it displayed the fact that it was composed of four big 'petals'. Thus the bomber came quite steeply out of the sky on a sort of flower-like parachute. Fascinating though this pattern was, it presented various problems, not the least of which was that it caused the rear of the fuselage to distort, and later in the war a new type of braking system was substituted, taking the form of slotted plates between the engine nacelles and the fuselage sides. As a dive-bomber, however, the Do 217 was not a conspicuous success. Nor, for that matter, was the even larger four-engined Heinkel He 177, the excessive weight of which was partly attributable to the great structural strength demanded for diving attacks. As on the Ju 88, the dive-brakes resembled farm gates – and were very nearly as large!

In developing specialised dive-bombers the Italians lagged somewhat behind the Americans, just as they did in the introduction of assault, or attack, aircraft. Nevertheless, they did produce and operate a single type, which, although it can hardly be classed as a success, demands more than a passing mention. This type was the Savoia Marchetti

◄ Sturdy in appearance and structure was Germany's Henschel Hs 123 single-seat biplane dive-bomber.

S.M.85, first tested in 1938 and distinguished in having twin engines, although it was only a single-seater. By this arrangement the pilot was able to sit well forward in the nose (where there was no engine as on the big bombers and torpedo-droppers of the same make) and thus to have an excellent view of his target, not merely over the tip of the fuselage but through a transparent panel in the cockpit floor.

Like many other Italian aeroplanes, the S.M.85 was largely of wooden construction, and although it weighed well over 9,000 lb (4,080 kg) (roughly the same as a contemporary Ju 87), it was less powerful, for the two Piaggio engines gave only 500 hp each. To facilitate accurate delivery of the standard load of one 550-lb (250 kg) or 1,100-lb (500 kg) bomb, dive-brakes were built in to the inboard trailing edges of the monoplane wing, which was set at the shoulder position on the angular-section fuselage.

Only one unit of the Italian Air Force was equipped with the S.M.85, and its Service life was short, for Ju 87s were made available as replacements.

By comparison with this unusual Italian machine, the Japanese dive-bombers were fairly conventional, and bore the names of Aichi, Kawasaki and Yoko-suka. The Aichi D1A was a biplane dating from 1933, and its interest stemmed largely from the fact that its origins were German, the equivalent type

being designated Heinkel He 50, which has received no previous mention because of its relative un-importance in Germany's technical programme. Sound in design and sturdy in construction, the Type D1A was developed by the Aichi company into the D1A2, the latter version appearing in 1936 and being involved in the international incident caused by the dive-bombing of the US gunboat *Panay* in the Yangtze river. Thus, the real interest of this German/Japanese biplane was more political than technical.

Yet the next Aichi dive-bomber, the D3A, was involved not only in the sinking of famous ships, including those at Pearl Harbor in December 1941, the British aircraft-carrier *Hermes* and the cruisers *Cornwall* and *Dorsetshire*, but was one of unusual technical interest also. In general outline, having typically Heinkel elliptical monoplane wings (the 'Spitfire shape' to British eyes), this type resembled the very beautiful He 118, which was an unsuccessful rival of the by no means beautiful Ju 87; yet the Japanese machine had a fixed undercarriage, which was a distinguishing feature of the latter type, and dive-brakes of an almost identical pattern. Thus the pedigree of this successful Japanese equivalent of the Douglas Dauntless was a very mixed one indeed.

The single Kawasaki type to be mentioned – the Ki-48 – was used for dive-bombing as well as level bombing, but the dive-bombing version had a special designation (Model 2B) as well as special equipment. This equipment was mainly in the form of retractable dive-brakes in the under-surfaces of the outer wings, but to improve directional stability in a diving attack a larger dorsal fin was another special fitment.

As with the Kawasaki company, so with Japan's Yokosuka Naval Air Arsenal, only one type of dive-bomber calls for mention, namely the D4Y, or Suisei (Comet). The name was an apt one, for this shapely two-seat carrier-borne, low-wing monoplane was capable of speeds around 360 mph (580 km/h), due in part to the 'clean' nose-shape allowed by

Probably the most handsome dive-bomber ever built was Japan's Yokosuka D4Y Suisei (Comet). The liquid-cooled engine accentuated its fine lines.

the twelve-cylinder liquid-cooled engine, whereas the Japanese Navy (like that of the United States) generally favoured the air-cooled type. The original engine, however, presented various difficulties, and an air-cooled design was later substituted. Later still, rockets were fitted under the fuselage to improve take-off from small aircraft-carriers.

The procedure for taking-off from ships could be either direct (under the aircraft's own power), with rocket assistance, as instanced by the Suisei, or by catapult; but a type of airborne, rather than sea-borne, carrier was a Russian Tupolev TB-3 bomber. Carrying two bomb-laden Polikarpov I-16 monoplane fighters under its wings, one of these big four-engined monoplanes was employed during 1941 for an attack on an important bridge over the River Danube; but although all members of the three-aircraft team returned safely from this astonishing raid it was never repeated.

That the dominant Russian strike aircraft of the Second World War was the low-flying, heavily armoured Stormovik has already been made clear; dive-bombers were, to the Russians, of secondary importance. Yet when the Germans invaded the Soviet Union they had in service a number of such aircraft, designated Archangelskii Ar-2, though these were merely adaptations of the vastly more famous level-bombing Tupolev SB-2, having smaller wings incorporating dive-brakes. In any case, both types were superseded by the Petlyakov Pe-2, which, although originally tried as a high-altitude level bomber, was developed for diving attacks by adding braking surfaces under the wings.

After the pioneer experiments of 1917, nothing of any real consequence was done in Britain's development of dive-bombers until the 1930s were well advanced, when the Hawker Hart and Hind biplanes and Fairey Battle monoplanes of the RAF began to practise attacking in a dive as well as on the level. Before the advent of the Blackburn Skua, in fact, there existed only a single British machine which could reasonably be called a 'real' dive-bomber, and even this, as its designation Hawker P.V.4 implied, was a private venture, in the design of which such diverse official requirements as army co-operation and torpedo-dropping were studiously ignored. Production orders were not forthcoming.

It is fitting to mention at this point that biplanes, and in particular the big, sturdy single-engined torpedo-droppers, well exemplified by the Vickers Vildebeest and Fairey Swordfish, proved, in their way, very suitable for dive-bombing, for, such was the profusion of struts and other air-resisting items (not least the crew, who had no roof to their heads) that no special brakes were required. So slowly, indeed, did these dependable if graceless machines

gain speed when the nose went down that neither the structure nor the pilot's airspeed indicator was ever likely to be overstressed.

A very different proposition was the Blackburn Skua, for not only was this the first monoplane to enter service with Britain's Fleet Air Arm (1938), but it had a retractable undercarriage and enclosed crew accommodation also, and was capable of well over 200 mph (320 km/h) in level flight. Flaps fitted on the wings served not only to steepen the gliding angle and reduce the landing speed for operation from an aircraft-carrier's deck but to limit speed in a bombing dive, the bomb delivered being a single 500-pounder, stowed partially in a shallow recess in the fuselage and provided with displacement arms, following American practice. The fact that there were four fixed machine-guns in the wings as well as a fifth at the rear, the intention being that the Skua should serve for fighting as well as dive-bombing, is incidental to the present narrative; but one event that must be recorded to the credit of this often-maligned aeroplane is the sinking of the German cruiser *Königsberg*. After the war was over the Skua's designer remarked: 'Our only regret was that we were not allowed to go ahead with a simplified version with fixed undercarriage as a first-class dive-bomber for the Air Force as an answer to the German Stukas.'

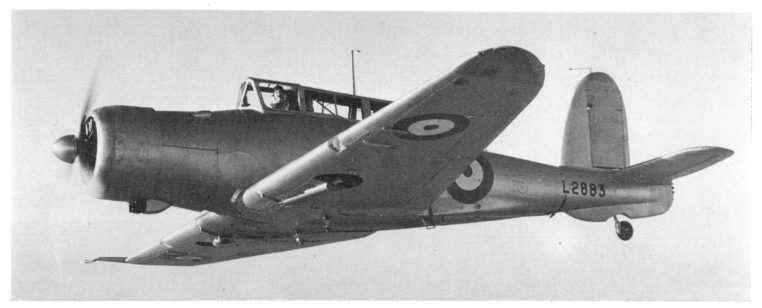

The Blackburn Skua was the first British dive-bomber to be fitted with dive-brakes, and carried a single 500-lb bomb in a recess in the bottom of the fuselage.

Wings and flaps having just figured so prominently, this record of dive-bomber development may be appropriately concluded by referring again to the Fairey Barracuda, already named as a torpedo-carrier. On this monoplane the very large flaps served the same purposes as those of the Skua, but, being fixed below and behind the rear edge of the wing, made the Barracuda appear from some viewpoints to be almost a sesquiplane, or 'one-and-a-half-winger'. Their braking effect was put to use when Barracudas struck at the battleship *Tirpitz*, using 1,600-lb (725 kg) bombs; and though the strikes were unsuccessful they were evidence of growth in hitting power.

Mainly because of its vulnerability to fighter attack and to increasingly effective anti-aircraft gunnery the dive-bomber was eventually succeeded very largely by the fighter bomber, a class which, though it originated in the 1914–18 war, has yet to be accorded its highest honours.

	Span	Length	Crew	Loaded weight	Maximum speed	Armament
USA						
Curtiss F8C-4 Helldiver	32' 1"	25' 11"	2	4,367 lb	138 mph	Bomb(s)+4 m-g
Martin BM-1	41' 0"	28' 9"	2	6,259 lb	145 mph	Bomb(s)+2 m-g
Douglas SBD-3 Dauntless	41' 6"	32' 8"	2	10,400 lb	250 mph	Bomb(s)+4 m-g
Curtiss SBC-4 Helldiver	34' 0"	27' 6"	2	7,141 lb	237 mph	Bomb(s)+2 m-g
Curtiss SB2C-1 Helldiver	49' 9"	36' 8"	2	16,607 lb	281 mph	Bomb(s)+6 m-g or 2 cannon+2 m-g
GERMANY						
Junkers Ju 87B	45' 3"	36' 5"	2	9,370 lb	232 mph	Bomb(s)+3 m-g
ITALY						
Savoia Marchetti S.M.85	45' 11"	34' 5"	1	9,237 lb	228 mph	Bomb(s)+1 or 2 m-g
JAPAN						
Aichi D3A1	47' 1"	33' 5"	2	8,047 lb	242 mph	Bomb(s)+3 m-g
Yokosuka D4Y2 Suisei	37' 9"	33' 6"	2	9,596 lb	360 mph	Bomb(s)+3 m-g
GREAT BRITAIN						
Blackburn Skua	46' 2"	35' 7"	2	8,228 lb	225 mph	Bomb+5 m-g

m-g = machine-gun

◀ A pair of Swedish Air Force Saab B17 dive-bombers.
The type first flew in 1940.

6

History Made and Repeated

The fact that a fighter, or any other aeroplane, parked on the ground is a sitting target which does not return gunfire from the air, and is extremely vulnerable even to the fragmentation, or anti-personnel type of bomb as delivered, for example, by the Camel and S.E.5a single-seaters of 1917–18, was still recognised in 1939, although the built-in bomb-carrying capability for aircraft of this class had lapsed with the Gloster Gladiator of the mid-1930s. But as fighters were adapted for bombing in the Second World War the 'demolition' or 'general-purpose' bombs employed quite commonly weighed 250, 500, or even 1,000 lb (113, 225 or 450 kg), and offensive capability was still further increased by rocket projectiles and by the use of napalm. The employment of napalm in a kind of incendiary bomb with fearful power to destroy or incapacitate, orig-

inated with the dropping of auxiliary fuel tanks by long-range fighters, though a chemical was added to the petrol to jellify it. The name 'hell jelly' was by no means a dramatisation.

To list all the single-seat fighters that were employed as fighter bombers in the war of 1939–45 for ground-attack with bombs as well as guns would be pointless, and there is, in fact, far more point in remarking that among all the numerous types of this period there were practically no exceptions.

Special mention must be made, however, of the Hawker Typhoon which achieved its greatest fame as a ground-attack aircraft. The history of this aeroplane is one of uncommon interest, though it is not exclusively glorious, for many troubles were encountered, and in its intended rôle as a super-

◀ Even without underwing bombs or rocket projectiles the Hawker Typhoon looked every inch a strike aircraft, especially so with its projecting 20-mm cannon and black and white 'invasion markings', as shown.

fighter the 'Tiffie', as it was known, proved in some important respects a disappointment. Yet this very aeroplane was to come to the notice of the British public with much the same acclaim as the entire German nation was made aware of the deadly Stuka, and the Russian people were sustained in their struggle by the exploits of the Stormovik.

The Typhoon was developed more or less in parallel with an even less successful Hawker fighter called the Tornado, both types being intended to surpass the Hurricane in every important respect, and to a very high extent indeed. Like the Avro Manchester twin-engined bomber, the Tornado was chosen to receive the massive Rolls-Royce Vulture engine, which proved a disappointment in itself. But whereas the Manchester was quite readily adaptable to take four Merlins in place of two Vultures, thus becoming the almost incredibly successful Lancaster, the Hawker fighter was (like all British fighters of the period except the Westland Whirlwind and a Gloster prototype) strictly designed around a single engine. Consideration was given in turn to several types of alternative powerplant – including one, called the Fairey Monarch, of which very few people have ever heard; but cancellation of the Vulture programme spelt also the abandoning of the Tornado; and so the Typhoon remained.

Among all the interesting facts in the Typhoon's history are several which concern its engine; for this was one which had much in common with the aeroplane it powered. It was mighty in terms of horsepower delivered, as the Typhoon was in striking power; it showed some very awkward teething troubles; it was not a brilliant performer at great heights; and it was hurried into service somewhat prematurely because of pressing need. As a piece of mechanism this engine – the Napier Sabre – was an engineer's dream, though it had no fewer than twenty-four cylinders to deliver its 2,000-odd horsepower. These cylinders were arranged in four banks, or rows, of six, in the frontal form of an H lying flat on its side, the cross-bar, of course, representing the crankcase. Thus the Sabre was a 'flat' engine, and so, in theory at least, should allow the pilot a good view forward over the nose. This facility, it can hardly be over-emphasised, is a requirement equally important in a strike aircraft as in a fighter. However heavy a boxer's punch, it is hopeless for him to enter the ring unless he can see quickly and clearly opposing threats and openings for attack. As the design of the Typhoon worked out on the Hawker drawing-boards, the pilot's view was nothing extraordinary, as it was, for instance, in the Whirlwind, with its twin, slim engines on the wings; but it sufficed, and Typhoon pilots were able to see their way to inflict a lot of punishment.

Strike loads carried by the Hawker Hurricane at various times included machine-guns, cannon of 20-mm or 40-mm calibre, rocket projectiles and bombs. These last could be of 250 lb, as seen, or 500 lb.

The first Typhoon was flown early in 1940, having been ordered in the summer of 1938. As already intimated, it was not an altogether lovable machine. For one thing, the Sabre engine, with a huge propeller to absorb the power, was mounted very close to the roots, or inner portions, of the over-thick wing, and this had the effect of setting up severe vibration. Clearly, this would not be conducive to accurate aiming of the guns – still less of the rocket projectiles, which were not even in prospect when the aircraft was designed. On take-off there was a most unpleasant tendency to swing, or slew; the rate of climb fell short of Fighter Command's hopes; and development was further hampered by very heavy demands for more and better Hurricanes. Even when the type finally entered service late in 1941, troubles were so persistent that there was serious thought of withdrawing it altogether, and the best that could be said for the new super-fighter was that it was fast enough at low level to catch the extremely troublesome German Focke-Wulf Fw 190 'tip-and-run' fighter bombers. Thus did a strike-aircraft-to-be deal with one that was already establishing itself as a new and significant threat.

Although, in their earlier days, the Typhoon and its engine showed some highly disagreeable characteristics – to which might be added the terrifying one of structural failure in a dive – the time has come to relate how Hawker's hefty fighter achieved its ultimate fame, together with its less troublesome development the Tempest. The story concerns not only aeroplanes and engines but one solitary pilot whose name – Wing Commander Roland Beamont – is identified with the operation, testing and development of British strike aircraft.

After acquitting himself with success and gallantry in the Battle of Britain, Beamont reported during 1942 to the Hawker factory at Slough. His assignment was that of test pilot for run-of-the-mill Hurricanes. This was the type he had flown in the Battle, and of which he once said: 'If the Hurricane was an inferior fighter in the Battle of Britain, nobody told the pilots.' Beamont was persuasive, and it took him little time to get himself transferred to the 'intensive flying' phase of Typhoon testing. Soon he began to hanker after some more fighting, and it transpired that from October 1942 to the spring of 1943 he was flying Typhoons in anger, mainly against the tip-and-run intruders. Under the code-name 'Rhubarb', Fighter Command had begun low-level bad-weather operations over France and Belgium against 'targets of opportunity' on the ground. Hurricanes and Spitfires were the types in use, but Beamont was by now a Typhoon enthusiast and, with its built-in armament of four 20-mm cannon, saw in the new if still-troublesome fighter a deadly machine for ground attack.

Beamont's personal account of his flying career *Phoenix into Ashes* contains his own first-hand description of early Typhoon strikes. Thus:

'In two night raids I hit four trains, and in seven more day and night attacks hit eight trains with impressive results. Defensive fire was considerable and this soon became a problem.

'There was at first little apparent enthusiasm from the pilots for this activity and I did not press

it until I had had a chance to establish the principle, but when it became clear beyond doubt that the Typhoon could be used with ease to winkle out pin-point targets on the ground by day or night and then attack them with accuracy and effect I decided to extend the operation and put up a roster of pilots for day and night ground attack training . . .'

Then, of an actual attack:

'The armourers talked over the state of the guns and the gun-sight, especially as at this time we had illegally modified a G.M.2 reflector sight to reflect directly on to the windscreen . . . a very valuable aid to night attack vision as it proved to be . . .

'The attacks developed into an almost standard pattern – landfall check; new course to target area; pick-up railway line (or airfield); dive, turn, and climb away from flak or searchlights; then the revealing plume of steam from a train (sometimes troop trains actually time-tabled for us by Fighter Command Intelligence); a throttled-back dive to line up and begin the attack before the tell-tale steam was cut off; the flashes of one's first shells bursting near it enabling quick correction of aim whilst straining to hold the misty, almost invisible target in the gun-sight; the shower-of-sparks effect of machine-gun tracer return fire or the bright balls of 40-millimetre tracer that seemed leisurely enough at source only to whip by with vicious shock-waves

The title of one official, confidential, and memorably ▶ light-hearted RAF publication intended for the instruction of pilots in launching rocket projectiles was *The Rocket Racket*. Its contents had doubtless been digested by the pilot of this clipped-wing Spitfire.

that could be felt sometimes when very close . . . All these became routine . . .'

To this vivid account only three footnotes need be added for the reader: first, the G.M.2 reflector sight was the luminous type as used in the Battle of Britain; second, 'flak' was the internationally accepted German contraction for anti-aircraft fire; third, tracer was a type of ammunition which visually traced the path of a shell or bullet.

As a strike aircraft the Typhoon was now a proven and a potent weapon; but its great engine power and lifting ability clearly invited the supplementing of the cannon by bombs. Originally these were two of 250 lb (113 kg), but this external load was progressively increased to two of 500 lb (225 kg) and eventually a pair of 1,000-pounders (450 kg). But it was as the 'rocket-firing Typhoon' that the British public and the world at large came to regard it with awe and affection. The rockets were eight in number, carried on long and massive launching rails, four beneath each wing. The projectiles themselves had long bodies, with stabilising fins at the rear and at the tip a warhead, or container for explosive, measuring 3 in (75 mm) in diameter and weighing 60 lb (27 kg).

The year in which the '60-lb RP' achieved its fame was 1944, when some of the fiercest battles in the history of warfare were being fought in France as a prelude to, and a decisive part of, the Allied invasion launched on 6 June of that year.

By the public the Typhoon was – and continues to be – held in the highest regard as a 'tank-buster', because of the mauling it gave the German Panzer divisions. But wars of such a magnitude are not entirely won by knocking out opposing weapons: the turn of events may almost equally be influenced by eliminating the key men of the General Staff, whose decisions determine the disposition and employment of those weapons. Thus it came about that on 24 October 1944 five squadrons of Typhoons devastated the Headquarters of the German Fifteenth Army with 500-lb (225 kg) and 1,000-lb (450 kg) bombs, killing more than seventy staff officers. There were similar assaults on key personnel, but on one particular sortie the target was a single key person – none other than General Rommel himself, wounded while riding in his big Mercedes.

After a Mercedes, a cab-rank may appear as something of an anti-climax; yet in the story of the Typhoon this is far from being the case, for cab-rank was the name acquired by the 'standing patrols' of these aircraft which ranged over the battlefields waiting for radio calls from the hard-pressed soldiery to deal with some of the most difficult targets. And so the Typhoon became a forerunner of our now-familiar radio cabs.

The Hawker Tempest was a successor to the Typhoon, and that it possessed a similar aptitude for striking at ground targets is evident in this picture.

From ranging the battlefields to heading out hundreds of miles over the lonely Atlantic brings not only one of the abruptest changes of scene that can be imagined but vastly different tasks and equipment. One solitary type of aeroplane is here concerned, the Focke-Wulf Fw 200 Condor, and there are doubtless many people who would contend that even this has no rightful place in a book about strike aircraft, and that it would be more fittingly considered in company with the great ocean-patrol machines like the Short Sunderland flying-boat and a series of efficient landplanes which have culminated in the Hawker Siddeley Nimrod. Yet the tasks of such machines are various, and numbered high

In its time – from early in the Second World War, that is, until 1942/3 – the Focke-Wulf Condor, a four-engined landplane with a span of well over 100 ft, was a highly successful anti-shipping strike aircraft. The 20-mm cannon seen here supplemented various combinations of bombs and machine-guns.

among them is the detection and destruction of submarines. On the other hand, the Condor made a particular practice of co-operating with submarines, and had such a singleness of purpose, and entered the war at such a critical phase, that it commands recognition and respect as a specialised strike aircraft for use against merchant shipping. In this sense it was the first famous airborne sea-raider of all – and it was nothing more or less than a con-

verted passenger-carrier! This graceful four-engined monoplane was an outstanding German transport and it was the first aircraft of its kind to fly the North Atlantic. The present writer recalls a captured Condor captain describing his great aeroplane as the 'tinfoil bomber', for its structure had been designed solely for staid civilian employment, and the Condor was never numbered among those German military types planned, tongue-in-cheek, as 'mail-carriers' or 'high-speed airliners'.

Armament was certainly not impressive – a few machine-guns placed as convenient, a 20-mm cannon, and from one to four 550-lb (250 kg) bombs; but not without reason did Winston Churchill dub the Condor 'the scourge of the Atlantic'. It was a preeminent instance of adaptation; and adaptability is a quality that largely forms the theme of this entire chapter, although it is devoted to some of the most famous aeroplanes of the Second World War.

Between adaptation and misemployment, however, massive possibilities for error exist, and in the entire history of warfare, whether by land, sea or air, nowhere is this fact more evident than in the epic instances of the 'Dambusting' raids by RAF Avro Lancasters and the USAAF attacks on the Rumanian oilfields, using Consolidated B-24 Liberators. In both these low-level strikes the aircraft concerned were large four-engined machines de-

No more dramatic contrast between the single-seat fighter bombers of the Second World War and the great four-engined bombers that were employed on exceptional occasions for low-level attacks could be presented than this shattering view of a Consolidated B-24 Liberator in action over the Ploesti oilfields.

signed essentially for high-level bombing; but whereas the Lancasters operated by night, using special tactics and techniques to deliver a very special type of secret weapon – the Wallis 'spinning-drum' or 'bouncing' bomb – the Liberators attacked in daylight and, despite intensive training and a minor application of special equipment, presented in mass such a target that it could hardly be expected to escape decimation. Moreover, a round trip of some 2,000 miles (3,200 km) was involved, and the fact that, of 179 machines despatched, no fewer than 53 were lost, came as a grievous justification of misgivings and warnings expressed beforehand by officers experienced in low-level operations.

While it is true that big multi-jet bombers today are regularly operated near the ground, the environment is quite a different one. Against forewarning by radar, low height is, in itself, protection, and radar countermeasures are not by any means a new development; yet the fact remains that any big aeroplane, even when flying alone and at speeds approaching that of sound, is vulnerable, and particularly so to the latest types of specially designed low-level anti-aircraft missile.

The development and activities of the Hawker Typhoon have received early attention, for this aeroplane was the pre-eminent example of its class; and likewise noted were the depredations of the

German tip-and-run raiders, for these afforded classic examples of the 'lightning strike'. So fast, in fact, was the Fw 190 (even with its bomb in place, and especially after diving) that even a defending Typhoon pilot was caused to reflect that he always seemed to be going downhill! An American pilot, on first seeing a Republic P-47 Thunderbolt, which

Though British fighter bombers of World War Two launched their rocket projectiles from underwing rails, Thunderbolts and Mustangs of the USAAF were fitted with tubular launchers, as witness this close-up of a Thunderbolt, showing also the machine-guns in the wing.

was in terms of bulk a near-equivalent of the Typhoon, and was, in any case, so massive in relation to, say, a Spitfire or Mustang, that it acquired the name of 'Jug' (for Juggernaut), remarked that it looked 'more like a dive-bomber than a fighter'. In this seemingly facetious observation there was, in fact, real truth, for not only did the 'Jug' bear distinct points of physical resemblance to the Helldiver monoplane, but it was itself tried in a similar rôle, although such was its weight and cleanness of line that it gained excessive speed very quickly, for it had no dive-brakes.

The functions and the fame of the Thunderbolt were very largely shared in the European conflict by the Lockheed P-38 Lightning and the North American P-51 Mustang. Not only was a version of the Mustang fitted with dive-brakes but it was quite extensively used, though not with great success.

During the Second World War a record of the wings of USAAF and RAF aircraft damaged by telegraph poles, and propeller tips bent by hard substances such as earth, might, in its way, be almost as impressive as a count of aircraft, trains and other targets damaged or destroyed – not, of course, numerically, but certainly in terms of structural integrity and of determination to return to base.

Although aircraft and trains were favourite targets for low-flying attacks, it must not be forgotten that

Ram was the name of this particular type of heavy rocket projectile, shown during a test-firing from a US Navy Vought F4U Corsair, which, in general performance and capability, was an equivalent to the USAAF's Republic Thunderbolt.

there were some with tougher skins, demanding heavier ordnance in the form of big guns or rocket projectiles. The Ju 87, the most famous of all dive-bombers, was in its later life developed as a 'tank-buster', with a 37-mm cannon beneath each wing. In the RAF the Hawker Hurricane was called upon to perform a similar function with two 40-mm cannon, yet still retaining one tenuous association with the Battle of Britain in the form of two of its original eight Browning machine-guns which, firing tracer ammunition, served as 'sighters'. For limited anti-shipping use, the twin-engined de Havilland Mosquito carried in its nose a 57-mm six-pounder, as well as four machine-guns. But the highest honours – both technical and operational – must go to the North American B-25H Mitchell, which, with a 75-mm cannon in close association with fourteen 0·5-in machine-guns, made its presence felt and heard in the Pacific area.

Both the Mosquito and Mitchell belonged essen-

The North American B-25 Mitchell first flew in 1940, but, such was its general excellence and adaptability, that, just a few hours before these words were written, in July 1972, one was seen being used to take photographs over London. This particular photograph shows a Mitchell delivering a rocket projectile named Tiny Tim – its diameter being a mere 11·75 inches!

History Made and Repeated

tially to the class of twin-engined bomber used for low-level as well as high-level operation (the 'Mossies' attacked Amiens prison, for example, distinctly low); and to these must be added such types as the Bristol Blenheim, the Martin Maryland, Baltimore and Marauder, all under various designations, and the splendid family of Douglases, beginning with the DB-7 'attack bomber' of 1938, latterly known as the A-20 or Boston, and culminating with the A-26 Invader. Serving in the Korean War, the Invader, which reconciled speed and armament as no other aeroplane of its class had done before it, was re-designated B-26, thus signalling the final and official demise of the US 'attack' category and acknowledging the dominance of the bomb over massed machine-guns. Yet the Mitchell (such are the changing needs of war and the whims or perversities of planners) had similar origins; and though it served in the main as a specialised bomber – the famous B-25 – it has already been instanced as a super gun-carrier. Of even greater consequence perhaps, was a yet more astonishing application, for in April 1942 a force of sixteen B-25 landplanes took-off from the aircraft-carrier uss *Hornet*, for the valorous, if militarily insignificant, raid on Tokyo.

In the next, and final, chapter, wherein a reckoning will be made of what the term 'strike aircraft' means today, affinities will be instanced between

Among the famous Grumman 'cat' family of US Navy fighters and fighter bombers, the Hellcat was the most ferocious member to serve in the Second World War. This ferocity is accentuated here by a Tiny Tim rocket projectile.

this particular operation and the introduction of Britain's Blackburn Buccaneer, the first aeroplane in history with which the word 'strike' was associated as part of its official designation. That this present chapter is not concluded with a data-table is, perhaps, the best affirmation that it is one that deals with adaptation and change.

Seen from the air, the launching of rocket-projectiles was no less impressive than when viewed from the ground, as this rear view of an F-84 Thunderjet in action will affirm.

7

Striking Ahead from 1945

The remark was made in the previous chapter that it would be pointless to list all the single-seat fighters that were used during 1939–45, for ground attack with bombs as well as guns, for there were practically no exceptions. The same is true of the fighters of the post-war years, though three exceptions deserve mention for particular reasons. First the English Electric (later BAC) Lightning, which was regarded from its very beginning as a pure interceptor fighter, intended for nothing else than destroying other aeroplanes in the air, yet which is seen today fairly bristling with assorted weapons for ground attack. Second, the shapely, but big and demanding, Republic F-105 Thunderchief, which in many ways can be regarded as a jet-propelled descendant of the P-47 Thunderbolt. It has been described as a 'one-man air force' and this stems not so much from the considerable bodies of specialist personnel required to maintain its complex electronic weapon-delivery systems in fighting trim as from its astonishing ability to carry much the same bomb load as a four-engined wartime Flying Fortress, 12,000 lb (5,445 kg). Yet this big aeroplane has one seat and one engine only, and -- such is progress – has already been out of production for about ten years. Thirdly we have the McDonnell Douglas Phantom II, which, though surpassing the capabilities of the Thunderchief in its air-to-air fighting capabilities, nevertheless carries such a load of miscellaneous ordnance in the form of guns, bombs, rocket projectiles or air-to-ground missiles, that, in its own right, it must rank among the most effective strike aircraft of specialised design.

Yet all three of these types are, in truth, merely

This Republic F-84 Thunderjet scores a bull's-eye in a 'skip-bombing' event.

the modern counterparts of the fighter bombers which had their origins in the First World War; and of far greater importance in this particular book are not (as might be supposed) even bigger and better aircraft of this general class, but some relatively tiny aeroplanes that look like fighters, often behave like fighters in their aptitude for quick manoeuvre, and are still persistently alluded to as

fighters – but, for all this, are, beyond question, *strike aircraft*. The first, and by far the most widely used, of these capable little machines is the Fiat G.91, which looks, in its original and best-known form at least, almost exactly like a shrunken North American Sabre fighter, though it has latterly been developed with two jet engines instead of one and thus has broadened a little in the beam. The greatest distinction of the G.91 is that it was chosen as long ago as 1957 as the standard 'tactical' aircraft for countries of the North Atlantic Treaty Organization, the word tactical merely signifying in this instance, that, in addition to its primary task of ground attack, it can be used, in modified form, to reconnoitre for the army.

Directly competing with the G.91 was an appealing little French machine called the Dassault Étendard, which, though unsuccessful in securing massive NATO orders, rendered, in developed form, excellent service as a carrier-borne fighter bomber with the French Navy. But far more remarkable in many ways was a comparable and contemporary American Navy type, the Douglas Skyhawk; and the most remarkable of its physical features was its wing span of a mere 27 ft 6 in (8·38 m). So ingenious was the design of this little aeroplane that it reconciled excellent flying qualities and the stringent demands of carrier operation with a most impressive weapon capacity, varying greatly according to version, range and type of target. Numbered among its possible weapons (as on the Phantom II and other types of low-level strike aircraft, including the wartime Ju 87) were 'gun pods', or packages, of machine-guns readily attachable beneath the wings. Of far greater operational significance, however, were two added features, both of which proved

vital to the successful and confident functioning of later and larger strike machines and which were known respectively as terrain-clearance radar and the low-level ejection seat, for emergency crew-escape.

The Skyhawk was known to those who built it as 'Heinemann's Hot Rod', after its designer Ed Heinemann, but was to become even more familiar as the 'bantam bomber'. Deletion of the word fighter was not merely in the interests of alliteration

The first point to appreciate concerning this group-portrait of a McDonnell Phantom II with its assortment of warlike 'stores' (as such items are technically known) is that they are not all carried simultaneously. Very numerous combinations are, however, possible.

and convenience: it meant that, with the Skyhawk, the single-seat, jet-propelled, carrier-borne strike aircraft had now arrived. Such, indeed, was its all-round excellence and value for money that the type was adopted, for example, by Israel, a nation which does not number aircraft-carriers among her forces.

Today the best-known names among the smallest types are Hawker Siddeley Harrier and SEPECAT Jaguar. It is therefore necessary to introduce one final link with the fighter class of aeroplane, in the name of Corsair. This is a name that invites greater confusion even than Helldiver, for it was first applied by the American Vought company to a series of two-seat biplanes in the 1930s, was later transferred to the famous single-seat fighter bomber of the Pacific and Korean Wars, but is now familiar, as Corsair II, in designating a smaller, lightweight development of the Ling-Temco-Vought Crusader fighter bomber but without the variable-incidence wing.

If an aeroplane having a variable-incidence wing, enabling it to reconcile a high performance in the air with the ability to operate from confined spaces, can be described as unusual, then one that has the ability to take-off and land vertically may in respect of strike aircraft be termed 'revolutionary'. Such an aeroplane is the Hawker Siddeley Harrier, which, although still rightly regarded as absolutely novel,

The Hawker Siddeley P.1127, or Kestrel, had all the essential characteristics of the much-improved present-day Harrier. As shown by this view of a P.1127 aboard the aircraft-carrier HMS *Bulwark*, machines of this class are eminently well suited for operation from ships as well as shore.

nevertheless dates back to the earliest tethered hovering tests, on 21 October 1960, of the Hawker P.1127. To remark that the P.1127 was, in a purely historical sense, the Harrier's true prototype, is per-

◀ Like its ancestor the Hurricane, the jet-propelled Hawker Hunter was an adaptable machine. The nearest specimen carries auxiliary underwing fuel tanks; the leader and the aircraft at the bottom respectively, tanks and rocket projectiles and tanks and bombs; while the odd-man-out carries nothing – except the two built-in 30-mm cannon!

fectly correct, for all the essential technical features were present; but an immense amount of development has meanwhile taken place, respecting not only structural and aerodynamic design and power-plant characteristics also, but especially in strike capability. A fact which is, perhaps, too little realised is that only some 5 per cent of the drawings are common to both types; yet potential for development remains immense, and as this book nears its completion there is serious talk of a joint Anglo/ American supersonic version, although, as it already exists, the Harrier attains over 720 mph (1,158 km/h) on the level, and in a dive exceeds the speed of sound by 25 per cent. Having a wing span of only about 25 ft (7·6 m) it is the most compact machine of its class, for it depends for lift not so much on its little wing as on its vectored-thrust (or twisting-nozzle) Rolls-Royce Bristol Pegasus turbofan engine. Wing-lift is useful, however, when the Harrier takes-off with a short forward run to carry the maximum possible load of fuel and weapons.

Though much has been written about the Harrier, its capability for sheer surprise is often overlooked, though this is a quality which was instanced at the very beginning as being a dominant one in any successful strike aircraft, whether in the nature of speed, manoeuvrability, silence, or near-invisibility. It is true that mobility of base has been frequently instanced as one of the Harrier's peculiar assets; but the very nature of the base itself is what concerns us here, for this aeroplane surprises in an entirely new way. Though it is little given to dodging round, or hiding behind, clumps of trees to screen its approach or cover its escape, like its ancestor the Sopwith Camel, it is uniquely adept (for comparable Soviet types exist merely in experimental, and not operational, form) at concealing itself in, and literally jumping out of, a natural feature of this sort. It is hardly less at home on board ship and, whatever the future may hold for this particular strike aircraft, the type must be placed on record as one of the greatest – if not the greatest of all – technical advances since Marix's raid on the Zeppelin shed in a Sopwith Tabloid.

The twin-jet, single-seat SEPECAT Jaguar, as built by, and ordered by, Britain and France, is of conventional, though advanced, design, and makes no severe demands either on the dimensions of its airfield or the nature of its surface. Several variants are in being or in prospect, and of a typical strike version it is officially declared: 'Depending on type of navigation equipment installed, a choice of attack systems is available, from a standard gunsight to an entirely self-computing system with head-up display'. An attack system is an electronic one that does much of the pilot's job for him, as in any truly

Although a trainer version exists, the Anglo-French SEPECAT Jaguar is essentially a strike aircraft, and not a trainer-conversion, like a number of even more economical types now in service.

modern strike aircraft, for approach to the target is not only fast, but seems the more so because of the very low level. A 'head-up' display of instrumentation is one that does not require the pilot to lower his eyes.

For work over the longer ranges it is usual to carry a second crew-man to assist with navigation and other tasks, the precise nature of which remains largely secret. The prime example of such a fighter bomber is the Phantom II; but a specialised two-seat (though single-jet) strike aircraft of uncommon merit was the Swedish Saab A32A Lansen, dating from the 1950s. The Swedes were especially proud, and doubtless thankful also, that such was Lansen's speed that, operating from a central base, it could strike a distant coastal or land target anywhere in their country within an hour.

The two-seaters just named now lead us to consider the larger types intended to deliver more massive loads over longer ranges and having the

The Saab A32A specialised strike aircraft of the 1950s, seen here, is just one of several fine military types built by the Swedish aircraft industry since 1945.

ability to fly at speeds approaching that of sound at very low level for sustained periods. The word 'sustained' implies not merely continued flight on a single mission but over years of service. Their structural strength must thus be immense, especially so as the air at low level is often turbulent as well as being dense.

Now, at last, we may introduce a strike aeroplane that was not only designed as one but was actually *called* one, the twin-jet, two-seat Hawker Siddeley (Blackburn) Buccaneer, which, though it exists to-day in three main variants, designated S.1, S.2 and ·S.50, and differing essentially in powerplant, nevertheless share the common denominator of S for strike. That batches of Buccaneers have been acquired by the RAF and the South African Air

Force also must not obscure the fact that this aeroplane was designed specifically for operation from aircraft-carriers. After all, the motto of the Fleet Air Arm is *Find, Fix and Strike*, and with the Buccaneer the Navy was striking out not only against potential enemies but very strongly on its own behalf, for this is an aeroplane to meet definite, and clearly envisioned, naval requirements. In former times the Navy had frequently had to be content with mere adaptations of land machines – even, to be truthful, with types that no one else wanted.

The Buccaneer changed all this in 1958, and to British eyes it was a very dramatic-looking aircraft with its highly accentuated, American-inspired 'Coke-bottle', or area-ruled, fuselage. This was a feature whereby the cross-sectional area of the wing and fuselage were so proportioned as to give minimum drag at speeds near that of sound. The inclusion of nuclear weapons in the varied range of armament carried inside the fuselage and under the wings must also be instanced as an American innovation; and today, whenever bombs are mentioned in connection with a strike aircraft of any variety, it may generally be taken that these may be of the atomic kind.

There exists today in the US Navy a carrier-borne near-equivalent of the Buccaneer, namely the Grumman Intruder, and the antecedents of this

Seen beneath the wings of this Hawker Siddeley (Blackburn) Buccaneer carrier-borne strike aircraft are four Martel air-to-surface missiles, jointly developed by France and Great Britain. Alternative under-wing loads are auxiliary fuel tanks.

type may be traced back to the Tokyo raid of April 1942, which was made by twin-engined B-25 bombers that were launched from an aircraft-carrier though designed to operate from land. These bombers were, in any case, the first big twin-engined machines to fly from a carrier's deck, and, although the bombs they dropped were of the conventional kind ('iron' bombs, as they are known today), the US Navy's own first equivalent carrier-borne aircraft, the North American Savage, designed in 1946, was planned to have 'strategic nuclear strike capability'. This meant that it could fly for relatively long distances with an atomic bomb; and it must here

be explained that, although a strike aircraft thus armed may approach its target at a very low level, it may deliver its nuclear bomb in what is called a LABS (low-altitude bombing system) manoeuvre, that is, at the beginning of a steep climb-away from the target area.

As at first designed the Savage not only resembled the B-25 in overall appearance, but likewise had two piston engines, though in the form in which it entered service late in 1949 there was an additional, jet, engine in the tail. The Savage was not a great success, and in the year in which it became operational the Douglas company designed a far more advanced twin-jet equivalent called the A-3 Skywarrior, which was developed into the even more familiar land-based bomber known as the B-66 Destroyer. The operational purpose and official classification of the Skywarrior is, perhaps, best conveyed by recording that the first unit to receive it was VAH-1, or Heavy Attack Squadron One. Thus was the term 'attack' perpetuated in the US Navy's vocabulary, and 'attack' was still the designated rôle for the Skywarrior's successor, the North American A-5 Vigilante.

To declare even today that the Vigilante is one of the most elegant aircraft ever designed can hardly be disputed, though the first orders were placed as long ago as 1956; and, far more than this, one of its design features at least, namely the wedge-shaped air-intakes to the two jet engines, are a feature of the astonishing Soviet MiG-23. Design ingenuity, moreover, is more than skin-deep, for not only are the ordinary bombs ejected rearwards, but the Vigilante's nuclear weapon has attached to it two fuel tanks, which, after their contents are exhausted, are released with the weapon to stabilise its path.

Although these features are described in the present tense, the Vigilante no longer serves in its primary rôle, but is used instead for reconnaissance and other duties.

Compared with this beauty the later Grumman Intruder, now extensively in service, is positively plain, and its frontal dumpiness is further accentuated when a special cabin is embodied to accommodate a crew of four for radar countermeasures. But low-level strike with a two-man crew remains a dominant requirement, and although this Grumman type may be no Diana among aeroplanes we nevertheless associate it with DIANE, for so named is the Digital Integrated Attack and Navigation system, the functions, if not the functionings, of which are thus expressed.

Intruder itself is a name of interest in our present narrative, for, without a capital I the word was applied in the 1939–45 war to aeroplanes that prowled by night to strike at targets of opportunity, and were closely associated in consequence with 'Rhubarb', as cultivated by RAF Fighter Command in the pre-Typhoon era. In post-war years the term intruder became once again familiar in the RAF with the adoption of special cannon-armed versions of the Canberra bomber, designated B(I)6 and B(I)8.

Any company which could produce an aeroplane having the incomparable merits of the Canberra, and could sell it to the USA, among numerous other nations, could hardly fail to succeed it with a type of no less technical distinction. Precisely this the English Electric (BAC) concern proceeded to do with its TSR.2, the initial letters signifying 'tactical strike and reconnaissance'; but although this was very much a strike aeroplane, having immense strength and elaborate equipment for weapon-delivery, the qualifying expression 'tactical' need not be taken over-seriously, for the TSR.2 was capable also of flying long distances on 'strategic' missions, and not merely short sorties in support of the army.

Abandonment of this magnificent aeroplane is generally accepted as having been on political and financial, rather than technical, grounds, for it was built only in prototype form.

An essentially comparable American type, how-

Although numerous difficulties and setbacks, both technical and financial, have attended the development of the General Dynamics F-111, seen here, several of its features, notably the variable-sweep wing, have been retained for the MRCA, or European multi-rôle combat aircraft.

ever, is in service today, although it has been frequently grounded by technical troubles. This fact is not altogether surprising, for the type concerned, the General Dynamics F-111, is the first operational aeroplane of any kind to feature a wing having variable sweepback, enabling it to land or take-off in less than 3,000 ft (915 m) and yet to achieve a speed of Mach 2·5 (that is, two-and-a-half times the speed of sound) at high altitude, or Mach 1·2 at sea level. It is this latter figure which gives an indication of the capabilities of a modern supersonic strike aircraft, and an aircraft of precisely this character is the MRCA (multi-rôle combat aircraft), components for which are very far advanced, as this book is written, in Great Britain, Germany and Italy. Hardly surprising, data concerning this aeroplane are secret, but although it will probably weigh

nearly 40,000 lb (18,145 kg), the span of its variable-sweep wing, when fully forward, is unlikely to exceed 40 ft (12·2 m). As the MRCA will probably not be in service before 1978, it may be necessary to wait some time for more specific details, especially concerning low-level strike capability.

Of recent Soviet developments there is little to say because little is known. As in other air forces, fighter bombers continue in use, and for specialised strike duties there is the Sukhoi Su-7, likewise serving in Czechoslovakia, Poland and the Arab Republic in Egypt. Though in function this type may be compared with the Fiat G.91, it is bigger and far more powerful – especially so when two jettisonable rockets are added to assist take-off from small airfields. As for the world-famous, yet still mysterious, MiG-23, dating though it does from about

For many years a standard type in the Soviet, and other, air forces, the Sukhoi Su-7 is an excellent example of an aeroplane which has all the essential characteristics of a fighter but is, in fact, a specialised strike aircraft.

A variable-sweep wing is not a feature of the Soviet MiG-23; but it is an exceptionally fine and fast aircraft. A strike version, or development, is considered possible, but little definite information is available.

1964, it need only be remarked that, although this super-fighter has a speed of Mach 3 at altitude, there is as yet only conjecture concerning its strike capability.

Classes of aeroplane which have no prominent place in this book despite certain relationships with classes reviewed, are, firstly, the converted trainers, which are economical both in cost and in room required for strike manoeuvres; then the 'gunships', which are big transport aeroplanes pressed into service as platforms for low-level mass machine-gunning; the so-called COIN, or counter-insurgency, machines, which have a particular interest because of their STOL (short take-off and landing) qualities, and, by no means least, the fixed-wing anti-submarine machines, now being joined or superseded by helicopters. The helicopter class of aircraft is, in fact, being extensively employed in Vietnam for attacking ground targets; but as an entire volume in this series has already been devoted to its characteristics and capabilities, no further allusion is needed.

Scant reference has been made, or even called for, to experimental types and projects, and anti-submarine aircraft are mentioned only incidentally. Their importance is, however, indicated in the preceding paragraph; but as fixed-wing types have ranged from tiny trainers to huge flying-boats, and as finding and fixing is now so vital that the strike may be a secondary consideration, they may for the present be dismissed with the remark that the dual rôles of hunter and killer, undertaken by the Grumman Guardian, eventually became merged in specialised types, among which the Fairey Gannet is historic.

	Span	Length	Crew	Loaded weight	Maximum speed	Armament
ITALY						
Fiat G.91	28' 2"	33' 9"	1	11,465 lb	670 mph	4 m-g or 2 cannon+ bombs or RPs
USA						
Douglas A-4 Skyhawk	27' 6"	39' 1"	1	15,000 lb	670 mph	m-g packs and/or bombs or RPs
North American AJ-1 Savage	75' 0"	65' 0"	3	55,000 lb	420 mph	Bombs
North American A-5 Vigilante	53' 0"	73' 2"	2	62,000 lb	1,385 mph	Bombs or gms
Grumman A-6 Intruder	53' 0"	54' 7"	2	60,626 lb	over 620 mph	Bombs or RPs or gms
GREAT BRITAIN						
Hawker Siddeléy (Blackburn) Buccaneer S.1	44' 0"	63' 5"	2	56,000 lb	over 650 mph	Bombs or RPs or gms
FRANCE/GREAT BRITAIN						
SEPECAT Jaguar	27' 10"	50' 11"	1	32,600 lb	1,120 mph	2 cannon+bombs or RPs or gms
USSR						
Sukhoi Su-7B	30' 0" approx.	over 50' 0"	1	Not known	over 1,000 mph	2 cannon+bombs or RPs

m-g=machine gun   RP=rocket projectile   gm=guided missile

FURTHER READING

Aircraft of the Royal Air Force since 1918, Owen Thetford, Putnam, London, 1972

British Aeroplanes 1914–18, J. M. Bruce, Putnam, London, 1957

British Naval Aircraft since 1912, Owen Thetford, Putnam, London, 1971

German Aircraft of the Second World War, J. R. Smith, Anthony Kay and E. J. Creek, Putnam, London, 1972

Japanese Aircraft of the Pacific War, J. R. Francillon, Putnam, London, 1970

Phoenix into Ashes, Roland Beamont, William Kimber & Co Ltd, London, 1968

United States Military Aircraft since 1908, Gordon Swanborough and Peter M. Bowers, Putnam, London, 1972

United States Navy Aircraft since 1911, Gordon Swanborough and Peter M. Bowers, Putnam, London, 1968

The World's Bombers, H. F. King, The Bodley Head, London, 1971

INDEX